CONTENTS

LIST OF TABLES

PREFACE

A number of individuals, researchers and PRO staff among them, have been kind enough to tell me how useful the earlier handbook, *Chancery Equity Records and Proceedings 1600–1800* (2nd edn.), has been. For myself, I can only say that the preparation of the present Exchequer equity handbook was facilitated by the lessons learned on the Chancery handbook. I was also generously supported once more by the Leverhulme Trust whose funding enabled me to appoint for two years an exceptionally qualified assistant, Dr Jessica Cooke, whose principal responsibility was to read and input the materials on the 860 cases that form the backbone of the research for this handbook.

Once again, the PRO provided space and hardware, and I am grateful for the support of Dr Aidan Lawes, Dr Elizabeth Hallam-Smith, and Dr David Thomas. My software needs were met by Dr Trevor Chalmers, building on his earlier efforts with respect to Chancery. In addition, the Institute of Historical Research wholeheartedly supported the project, not least by its sponsorship of the application for funding to the Leverhulme.

Colleagues were also generous with their advice and assistance. In particular, I should like to thank Professor Hamilton Bryson and Professors Robert B. Hume and Judith Milhous. Others who drew on their fund of knowledge about Exchequer equity and put me in their debt were Dr Amanda Bevan, Dr Richard Hoyle, Dr Patrick Polden, Dr Ruth Paley and Professors Nancy Mace and Margaret Hunt. Most of all, I am indebted to Miss Margaret Condon, whose knowledge of Exchequer materials in the PRO has proved an invaluable asset.

GLOSSARY

Administrator (Administratrix): court-appointed representative of one who died without making a will (*see also* Executor).

Affidavit: a voluntary written statement made under oath.

Amended Bill: *see* Bill (of complaint).

Answer: first pleading by the defendant. *See also* Demurrer, Disclaimer, Plea; also Cross Bill.

Attachment: initial process of contempt, normally to compel the party to enter bail for his/her appearance in court; attachment with proclamations issued if the initial process fails. *See also* Sequestration.

Bill (of complaint): initial statement of the plaintiff's case. The plaintiff, in light of the contents of the defendant's answer, might amend the original bill or, depending on the stage the suit had reached, might be required instead to file a supplemental bill if he wished to make changes. *See also* Cross Bill.

Bill (of review): petition, normally alleging an error in law, to reopen a case after a decree had been enrolled.

Bill (of revivor): petition to revive a suit which had abated because of the death of a party or other contingency such as the marriage of a female plaintiff.

Commission of Rebellion: process of contempt if attachment with proclamations failed; usually empowered sheriff to arrest the person in contempt. *See also* Sequestration.

Cross Bill: bill which a defendant was allowed to exhibit for the same cause against the original plaintiff, and thereby seek Discovery (*see below*) from the plaintiff.

de bene esse: evidence, usually in the form of Depositions, allowed provisionally but which could subsequently be ruled inadmissible.

Decree: judgement.

dedimus potestatem: commission authorizing persons to perform official acts outside of London and its immediate environs, such as the taking of a defendant's answer or the conducting of examinations of witnesses.

Demurrer: a pleading by defendant seeking discharge on grounds of lack of jurisdiction by the court or of technical insufficiency in the plaintiff's bill of complaint.

Deposition: witness's statement on oath, taken down in secrecy before an Examiner or commissioners under *dedimus potestatem*, in reply to written interrogatories prepared by the parties; depositions were supposed to be kept sealed until order for publication (*see below*). (Depositions might also be taken in Deputy Remembrancer's proceedings upon a reference.)

Disclaimer: express denial by a defendant that the matter in the plaintiff's bill concerned him/her in any way.

Discovery: securing of information from the opposing party, whether in the pleadings stage or the proofs stage.

Dismission: order, with the force of a decree, whereby a bill of complaint was dismissed (either for plaintiff's failure to proceed or because the Court adjudged the bill without merit).

Examination: the formal interrogation of witnesses (or parties) either prior to the hearing (the principal form of evidence in equity cases) or to elucidate matters of fact upon a reference to the Deputy Remembrancer. Usually, examination was by interrogatories and the testimony taken by writing, but an oral examination was possible at the hearing of a case under special circumstances (e.g., the authentication of documents).

Exception: formal allegation by a party that a defendant's answer or a Deputy's report was insufficient or in error, specifying the grounds for the exception.

Executor (Executrix): person(s) named by a testator to execute the provisions of his/her will.

Exemplification: certified and official copy of a document.

in forma pauperis: an arrangement whereby poor suitors were assigned legal representatives free of charge and allowed to proceed with their suits without the payment of official fees.

Injunction: an order of court requiring a party to take or to refrain from a certain course of action. The common injunction was to require the party to halt litigation in another court; the special injunction secured possession of property or restrained potentially irremediably damaging acts such as breach of copyright or waste; a permanent injunction might form part of a decree closing a case.

in perpetuam rei memoriam: depositions taken and kept out of the normal course as a means of preserving testimony from aged or sick persons or those leaving the realm.

Interrogatories: written questions formulated by the parties to put to witnesses to elicit their responses in writing (Depositions).

Interlocutory: matters arising in the course of a suit, notably proceedings on injunctions. *See also* Motion, Petition.

Motion: an oral application by a party's legal representative to the bench.

Order *nisi*: order unless (other party responds) – a provisional order.

Petition: a written application by a party's legal representative to the bench. In addition to petitions on procedural questions during the course of a suit ('ordinary' petitions), proceedings for a rehearing of an enrolled decree were initiated by a petition for review.

Plea: a response to a bill of complaint raising a point of law which, if upheld, would free the defendant from answering the bill.

Pleadings: formal preliminary statements by parties in suits including the bill of complaint and the various responses possible by a defendant. *See also* Replication, Rejoinder, Surrejoinder and Surrebutter.

Probate: certificate of the church court having jurisdiction over a deceased person's testament that it had been proved and might be executed.

Publication: when both sides in a suit had completed the examination of their witnesses, the Court would order the hitherto-sealed depositions to be opened for perusal and for the making of copies.

Reference: the referring by the Court to an official or other individual of matters related to the suit, most commonly for factual inquiry but also for mediation or arbitration.

Rejoinder: second pleading of a defendant's case, coming in response to the plaintiff's replication.

Replication: second pleading of a plaintiff's case, coming in response to the defendant's answer.

Sequestration: taking custody of property into the hands of the Court, either temporarily or for disposition.

subpoena: initial process of the Court requiring by writ that the defendant appear under penalty. Other versions of the writ could be used to enforce the attendance of a witness (*subpoena testificandum*) or to produce material evidences (*subpoena duces tecum*).

Supplemental Bill: *see* Bill (of complaint).

Surrejoinder and Surrebutter: third pleadings, respectively, of the plaintiff's and defendant's cases.

Terms: the legal year was divided into four terms: Michaelmas (roughly mid-October to late November); Hilary (mid-January to early February); Easter (early April to early May); Trinity (early June to early July). The long vacation ran from the end of Trinity term to the beginning of Michaelmas term.

NOTE ON FORM

All dates in the text and of documents are new style, with the year beginning on 1 January.

All documents cited in the text are from the Public Record Office (PRO) unless otherwise noted. In PRO terminology, documents are organized into series (heretofore, classes) denominated by letter codes for departments ('E' for Exchequer) and numbers; series into pieces which may be boxes, bundles or volumes; pieces, in turn, may be subdivided into smaller items (which may be as large as a box or as small as a single folio). A full ordering reference must contain at least three parts – the letter code, the series number, and the piece number, e.g. E 112/682. It may contain more parts, as in E 133/25/71 or in E 134/5W&M/Mich16.

As explained in the discussion of finding aids in Chapter Three, a 'list' or a 'listing' refers to a list of a series (usually piece by piece, sometimes by item), an 'index' usually refers to a modern fully-alphabetized list of the contents of all or part of a series, and an 'alphabet' is a listing (often the work of the officers of the Court) organized by suit title, i.e., by the first letter of the surname of the first plaintiff along with the surname of the first defendant (e.g., Smith v. Jones). In some important instances, Exchequer equity alphabets supply forenames as well as surnames and also list all the parties to the suit.

INTRODUCTION

A. The Court of Exchequer and its Jurisdiction in Equity

Compared to the Court of Chancery's history as England's premier jurisdiction in equity from the later fourteenth century onwards, the jurisdiction in equity of the Court of Exchequer is little known.[1] There are some good reasons for this: first, though Exchequer was functioning as a common law court from the early thirteenth century, its jurisdiction in equity only arose in the sixteenth century; secondly, even at its height in the later seventeenth and early eighteenth centuries, the volume of Exchequer's equitable business was substantially outstripped by that of Chancery; thirdly, whereas the Barons of the Exchequer not infrequently considered and often followed Chancery precedents, it was uncommon for Lord Chancellors to invoke holdings or practices of the Barons; and fourthly, the Exchequer's equitable jurisdiction was eventually in 1841 to be merged into that of Chancery.

Withal, the neglect of the Exchequer's equitable jurisdiction has been unfortunate. Above all, since nearly 100,000 suits were initiated in the Court during its two centuries of operation as a general jurisdiction in equity,[2] the researcher, especially in social and economic history and in family history, may overlook valuable and unique sources[3] – an omission potentially compounded by the fact that the profiles of litigants and subjects litigated differ significantly as between Exchequer and Chancery.[4] And in turn, these differing profiles may to a significant degree be linked with differences in the way the two Courts operated, including the fact, occasionally influencing the course of Exchequer equity proceedings, that this newer jurisdiction was yoked with its pre-existing responsibilities in royal revenue cases and also in the hearing of that general range of civil disputes that might alternatively be litigated before the other central common law courts, Common Pleas and King's Bench.

Certainly, the four Barons of the Court of Exchequer had a plethora of responsibilities in early modern England. Trained as common lawyers (and, from the mid-Elizabethan years, selected solely from among the pleaders who had been elevated to the rank of Serjeant), they exercised a common law jurisdiction in the Court's 'Office of Pleas' handling civil cases. In turn, along with the judges of King's Bench and Common Pleas (but in contradistinction to the Lord Chancellor and the Master of the Rolls), they twice yearly went on circuit throughout the realm to hold the assizes, hearing both civil and criminal cases.[5] At the same time, they

---

1 A noteworthy but isolated exception is W. H. Bryson, *The Equity Side of the Exchequer* (Cambridge, 1975, hereafter cited as Bryson). Bryson also has in preparation a volume of equity reports for the later 17th century, among them a significant number of unpublished Exchequer cases. See now also J. Milhous and R.D. Hume, 'Eighteenth-century Equity Lawsuits in the Court of Exchequer as a Source for Historical Research', *Historical Research* 70 (June 1997), 231–46; H. Horwitz, 'Chancery's "Younger Sister": the Court of Exchequer and its Equity Jurisdiction, 1649–1841', *Historical Research* 72 (June 1999), 160–82.
2 See Bryson, Appendix 1.
3 For some noteworthy finds in theatre and opera history, see Milhous and Hume, esp pp. 238–44. For other successful forays into Exchequer materials, see Chapter Four below.
4 These differences are documented and described below in Chapter Two.
5 For the impact of the Barons' circuit responsibilities on their proceedings in equity, see below Chapter Two.

exercised a distinctive jurisdiction – reflecting the Exchequer's primary function – in royal revenue cases, a jurisdiction exercised under the general authority of the King's Remembrancer.

Yet despite the many other demands on their attention, the Barons were to devote considerable time and effort to suits in equity during the seventeenth and eighteenth centuries: 'they took equity motions nearly every day the Court sat in term, and these motions had the precedence of the common law business'.[6] Moreover, 'they sat exclusively in Equity' for, 'I believe', 'two days in every week.'[7]

B. The Development and Expansion of the Exchequer's Jurisdiction in Equity

Initially, those privileged to initiate proceedings in equity before the Barons were royal officeholders and others having some connection with the collection and/or management of royal revenues, not excluding humble tenants on Crown manors. But if, with respect to litigants, the scope of Exchequer equity was initially 'more narrow and more specific' than the long-established jurisdiction of the Court of Chancery, from the outset the nature of the procedures the Barons followed and the remedies they offered were 'no different from the equity of the chancery'.[8]

In turn, the exclusion of all but specific types of litigants was ended during the troubled years of the mid-seventeenth century. Until then, litigants had to be privileged to take advantage of the equity jurisdiction of the Barons: that is, they had to have some genuine connection with the royal revenue – whether as royal officials, lessees or other holders of royal estates (i.e., as accountants to the Crown), or as debtors to the Crown. But from 1649 onwards, this connection persisted only as a fiction for many plaintiffs. On the one hand, the form of bills of complaint became increasingly standardized with plaintiffs now no longer specifying the office they held, the estate they leased, or the debt they owed the Crown. Rather, at first sporadically (and there are isolated instances in bills of the early and mid-1640s, too) and then almost universally from early 1649 onwards, plaintiffs, after stating their names and status and/or occupation, invoked the formula 'debtor and accountant' to the Commonwealth (after 1660, the Crown) 'as by the records of this honourable court and otherwise it doth and may appear', and then went on to propound the substance of their complaint. On the other hand, the Court during the 1650s and certainly thereafter refused (departing from past practice) to allow defendants to avoid answering the bill of complaint by countering in demurrer that the plaintiff was not *in fact* a debtor or accountant to the Crown.

The Court of Exchequer's assumption of a general equitable jurisdiction came at a moment of crisis in English history when the future of the law, both the common law and equity, was hotly contested. Not only was the legal system facing outspoken criticism for its delays, expense, and harshness (in matters of criminal offences), but also courts employing

---

6 Statement of Sutton Shore, barrister, at the House of Lords inquiry of 1840 on the Exchequer's equity jurisdiction: *Journals of the House of Lords*, vol. 72 (1840), Appendix 3: 'Administration of Justice Bill', p. 128, question 209. Hereafter cited as *JHL* 72.

7 *JHL* 72, 141, question 496 (statement of Baron Alderson).

8 Bryson, p. 13.

English bill procedure faced special challenges. The abolition of the Court of Star Chamber by act of the Long Parliament in 1641, to be sure, was in no small part a reaction to Archbishop Laud's use of that tribunal to harass and to punish critics of Charles I's policies in church and state. In addition, the judicial authority of the Privy Council was also removed by statute, while the Court of Requests, though not formally abolished, ceased to function in the early 1640s. Similarly, the regional councils of the North and of the Marches of Wales, both hitherto exercising busy equitable jurisdictions, were also swept away in the Long Parliament's attack on 'prerogative' legal institutions. Indeed, even Chancery, the principal court of equity, was not immune to challenge, in part by reason of guilt by association (Lord Keeper Finch was one of those impeached by the Long Parliament), in part by reason of its vulnerability to the more general grievances against the central royal courts of undue cost and delay.[9]

On the one hand, then, the upheavals of the 1640s offered opportunities to the Exchequer to take on a wider jurisdiction; on the other hand, it might be supposed – given the outcry against the central courts in general, and English bill jurisdictions in particular – that this was hardly a favourable climate for a major initiative by the Barons. Nor do the records of the Court throw a clear light on why or how its equitable jurisdiction came to be expanded at this juncture, though it seems likely that the dispersion of the royal lands was one impelling factor insofar as tenurial relationships on royal lands had been a major source of litigation on the equity side of Exchequer. In any event, the route that the Court followed is clear: simply, it ceased to look behind (or to allow defendants to challenge) the complainant's claim to be entitled to sue in equity in Exchequer – that is, the formal allegation with which bills of complaint began that he/she was a debtor or accountant to the Crown and hence entitled to invoke the Court's assistance in making good his/her claim (so as, the traditional rationale went, the individual might thereby be better positioned to pay what was owed to the Crown).[10] But the Court's records reveal no explicit decision to adopt this new course; we can only deduce it from its practice, and only gradually was the Court's new openness to suitors remarked by legal writers.

Since the Court expanded its jurisdiction without, apparently, either public announcement or the adoption of new rules, it is perhaps not surprising that recognition of this shift was slow in coming. The first reference in print to the innovation seems to have been in the manual *The Compleat Solicitor Performing His Duty* published in 1666: 'But now, whether the complainant be any way really priviledged or not, is not so much material; only he must suppose it in his Bill.'[11] Yet, already in 1656, the Court itself, in the case of Swan v. Porter, acknowledged in effect that it was formula, not substance, that was critical. In dismissing one part of the compound bill of complaint in Swan, the Court explained: 'the mother of the wife [the wife being the principal plaintiff and identifying herself as 'debtor and accountant'] ought

---

9 For the abortive reform of the Chancery in the 1650s, see the ordinance of 1654 (repealed 1658) in G. W. Sanders, *The Orders of the High Court of Chancery* (1845), pp. 254–72.

10 For instances of the Court's enforcement of this rule prior to the Civil Wars, see Bryson, p. 24.

11 Guildhall Library AN 15.3.37, p. 389. (Wing attributes this work, which went through at least four editions, to William Booth.) Neither the equitable jurisdiction of the Exchequer nor its recent expansion of jurisdiction was considered in the report of the 1651 commission for the reformation of the law (headed by Sir Matthew Hale) or in other reformist materials of the 1650s. However, it may be more than a coincidence that the first set of extant reports of Exchequer equity cases (the reporter, Thomas Hardres) dates from the 1650s.

to have been alledged debtor and accountant, else the court has no jurisdiction; and the reason is, because it is presumed that what is recovered must go in satisfaction of the debt owing to the King, and must therefore be alledged'.[12] In turn, in a work on law reform composed in mid-1665 but published only in the late eighteenth century, Matthew Hale (himself a Chief Baron during the 1660s) deplored the 'multitudes of English suits in the exchequer chamber' and urged that 'a stricter hand [be] used for the abridging of those suits to such only, as concern properly the king's revenue, the officers of the courts, and that were really debtors accomptants or fee farmers . . . for it is now apparent [most] are suits . . . concerning private persons and interests, wherein the king is little or nothing concerned; and all upon the fictitious titling of bills as debtors or accomptants, where there is really no such thing.'[13]

What began, then, as an unheralded innovation in the midst of political upheaval and clamour for the reform of the legal system (the Nominated Parliament of 1653 even resolved that the Court of Chancery should be abolished) survived the restoration of the monarchy and of the traditional order in state and church. Yet not all was reinstated in 1660. Although the Council of the Marches of Wales was resurrected (though abolished again in 1689), neither the Council of the North nor the Star Chamber nor the Court of Requests was revived. Thus, among the central courts, the broader equitable jurisdiction of Exchequer might appear to have been open to challenge by the Court of Chancery, but this was not a threat that materialized, at least in any sustained fashion, in the later seventeenth or the eighteenth centuries.

C. The Relations of the Court of Chancery and the Court of Exchequer

The reasons for successive Lord Chancellors' and Lord Keepers' apparent complacency at the expanded jurisdiction in equity of the Court of Exchequer can only be surmised. For one thing, as there had been little jostling for business among the various English bill tribunals of pre-Civil War England, so there appears in 1660 and in succeeding years no opinion discernible that there was anything awry or out of order in there being two central courts of equity with concurrent jurisdiction.[14] Rather, the Barons of the Exchequer 'allow all Bills and Answers, and other pleadings, and orders and decrees of the Chancery to be read for evidence, without any order for their allowance'.[15] Such a view may well have been reinforced by the fact that in the generation after 1660 both Chancery's and Exchequer's equitable business was growing in volume, in part because the pre-Civil War boom in litigation had not yet been

12 *The English Reports* (178 vols., Edinburgh, 1900–32); vol. 145, 380 (Hardres, 60). The Swans' original bill (signed by none other than Hardres), and the rest of the pleadings are to be found at E 112/306, no. 124. See also Charles Barton, *An Historical treatise of a Suit in Equity* (1796), p.16n: 'it is still however the practice, (and till lately was thought necessary) to alledge that the party aggrieved is indebted to the crown, and by reason of the injury complained of is rendered incapable of discharging that obligation.'

13 'Considerations touching the amendment or alteration of lawes', printed in *Collection of Tracts,* ed. Francis Hargrave (1787), I, 253–89, quotation at p. 278. See Bryson, p. 25 n.5, for the dating of this work.

14 Note Hale's endorsement in 'Considerations' of the concurrent jurisdiction of King's Bench and Common Pleas: 'it is reasonable that the subject may have a just election to proceed in either court, . . . and not be necessitated to sue in one, which in some cases . . . may be inconvenient', Hargrave, *Tracts,* p. 289.

15 [William Booth], *The Compleat Solicitor Performing His Duty* (1666), p. 403. This latitude did not, however, extend to depositions, even to ones that had been taken in the Exchequer for another suit.

checked, in part because both central courts of equity were now attracting business from the provinces that previously would have gone to the Council in the Marches of Wales and other more local tribunals with equity jurisdiction (among them the duchy court of Lancaster and the palatine court of Durham).[16]

To be sure, there survives clear evidence, in at least one instance, of persisting Chancery notions of superiority over the newcomer. In 1684, Lord Keeper Sir Francis North, faced with a prior suit in Exchequer to foreclose a mortgage and the mortgagor's subsequent bill in Chancery to redeem the mortgage, took umbrage at the mortgagee's plea that his suit in Exchequer should take priority as the earlier to be initiated. Not only did North deny the mortgagee's plea (with the extra burden of costs), but he went on to pontificate 'that Chancery was the highest court of equity and though, the Exchequer was an ancient Court of Equity, yet the same was but a private Court and its jurisdiction was only for getting in the King's Revenue, and for the King's Officers, and they ought to keep within their proper Bounds.' Moreover, in making his ruling against the mortgagee, North remarked ominously that 'there are several Precedents, that Injunctions have gone to the Exchequer in such Cases', though in fact none was issued in this instance.[17]

However, North's views (in some ways chiming in with Hale's earlier reservations about Exchequer's expansion of jurisdiction) were not apparently shared by his successors. Indeed, it is evident that by the end of the seventeenth century, the two courts were working together to hinder litigants from playing one off against the other principally by each according priority, as between the one and the other, to the forum in which a dispute was initiated. Thus, the papers of Sir Edward Ward reveal that early during his long tenure as Chief Baron (1695–1713) the two courts clarified this understanding with respect to situations in which a party in the later suit waived (or insufficiently pleaded) the priority in time of the suit pending in the other tribunal.[18]

The potential for controversy arose in the case of litigation begun in Chancery over the extraction of salt from the Droitwich (Worcestershire) pits. This was followed by a second suit, seemingly by different plaintiffs but in the same matter and against the same defendant (one Robert Steynor) in Exchequer.[19] Steynor did plead the pendency of suit in Chancery in a bid to halt proceedings in Exchequer but he failed to persuade the Barons. He then secured an injunction from Chancery inhibiting the progress of the cause in Exchequer. However, the Exchequer suit was allowed to proceed after an understanding was reached between Lord Keeper Somers and Ward (first broached in a conversation in the House of Lords on 12

---

16 For the decline of provincial equitable jurisdictions after the Civil Wars, see Henry Horwitz, *Chancery Equity Records and Proceedings 1600–1800* (PRO Handbook 27, 1998, hereafter cited as Horwitz, *Chancery Equity Records*), p. 39 and n.18.

17 Earl of Newburg v. Wren, 1 Vernon 220 @ *English Reports*, vol. 23, 427 (as Earl of Newbury v. Wren), and see also 1 *Eq. Ca. Abridged.* 134 @ *English Reports*, vol. 21, 938.

18 Ward's papers are in Lincoln's Inn Library, Miscellaneous manuscripts 511–40, 558–9. I am grateful to the Librarian Mr Guy Holborn for his courtesy and assistance.

19 In Chancery, the suit was brought by the bailiffs and burgesses of Droitwich against Steynor; in Exchequer, the plaintiffs were the Earl of Shrewsbury and other pit proprietors against Steynor. Steynor's allegation in Chancery was that the pit proprietors in Exchequer were themselves burgesses of Droitwich and so allies of the plaintiffs in Chancery; C 33/285, f. 66.

December 1696) – an understanding perhaps facilitated by the friendship and political links between the two men.[20] That agreement, as Ward minuted it in his papers[21], was that

> where soever there is or shall be priority of suit in either court, that if a bill touching the same matter shall be exhibited in the other court, and the party that is intitled to such priority will answer the suit in the other court and not insist upon the priority, or if he shall plead tendency of the suit in the first court and that plea shall be insufficiently pleaded and for that reason overruled (as it was in this) and the party shall so far submit to it to answer the bill or not to appeal to parliament for overruling such plea, that in all such cases or of the like nature the court where the priority of suit was will not grant an injunction . . . the party intituled to such priority having affirmed and submitted to the jurisdiction of the latter court.

On this basis, Somers resolved the imbroglio the following day by dissolving his earlier injunction, observing that to do otherwise might lead to a breach between the two courts.

As the two central courts of equity sought to avoid jurisdictional conflicts in the initiation of litigation, so the general rule between them was that a matter finally determined in one was *res adjudicata* in the other, save when the decree in question had been obtained by fraud.[22] Then, too, each court was prepared to cite the other's decisions. Not surprisingly, the citation of Chancery decisions by the Barons of the Exchequer was more frequent than the reverse, but this was not so much a function of any inferiority acknowledged by the Barons as it was the by-product of the much greater number of cases that the Chancery handled and its much longer history as a general jurisdiction in equity.[23] Nor was it any direct competition between the two jurisdictions that eventually led to the Exchequer's equity jurisdiction being merged with that of Chancery in 1841 by act of parliament. Indeed, as late as the 1820s, the enlargement of the Exchequer was being mooted as a partial solution to the log-jam of litigation in Chancery.[24]

D. The End of the Exchequer's Jurisdiction in Equity

The parliamentary decision of 1841 was taken in a not wholly dissimilar atmosphere to that which had prevailed in the mid-seventeenth century. In both periods, law reform and rationalization of the judicial structure were very much to the fore. In both, too, Chancery was a principal target of the reformers. But whereas in the 1640s, Exchequer had been largely ignored, in the 1830s it was the equitable jurisdiction of Exchequer that was especially vulnerable – a vulnerability deriving partly from its more limited volume of business and

---

20 Horwitz, 'Chancery's "Younger Sister"', p. 165, n. 24.
21 LI, Misc. Ms. 559, f. 31. Among the cause papers, Ward notes the dissolution of the Chancery injunction on Monday, 14 Dec.: LI, Ms. Misc. 515, f. 63v.
22 Bryson, p. 30, citing in particular Lord Chancellor Hardwicke's 1749 judgement in Barnesley v. Powell. See also the Chancery case of Wing v. Wing *(1724)* in 9 *Modern* 109 @*English Reports*, vol. 88, 347.
23 For occasional assertions in the eighteenth century of a residual superiority in Chancery, see Horwitz, 'Chancery's "Younger Sister"', p. 164 and n.19.
24 See fn. 29 below.

partly from a sharp drop in that business over the past two decades.

The decline in business began in the second decade of the nineteenth century. Whereas during the eighteenth century and up to 1810, the equity business of the Court had been far more important than its common law business, over the next quarter of a century that relationship was very nearly reversed.[25]

Exchequer's loss of equitable business from the late 'teens of the nineteenth century stemmed from successive parliamentary measures. The first was an Act of 1817 (57 George III c. 18), intended to speed-up the processing of Exchequer equity cases by abolishing the traditional practice of the four Barons hearing and deciding cases collegially, and providing instead for the hearing of Exchequer equity suits by the chief Baron alone. The effect of this legislation was unexpected: litigants seemed less ready to use Exchequer, wary of the results of having a single judge (and usually the same one) hear their case and then also review attempts to reverse unfavourable decisions in the initial proceeding.[26] The second was the Insolvent Debtors' Act of 1820 and its successor of 1826 (1 George IV c. 119 and 7 George IV c. 57) which by creating a court of bankruptcy had the result of diminishing the tide of 'common injunction' suits to the Exchequer.[27] And the third was the Tithe Commutations Act of 1836 (6–7 William IV c. 71), which had the effect of accelerating the decline of tithe litigation – a one-time staple in the Exchequer.[28] Yet if in retrospect the demise of Exchequer's equity jurisdiction may seem foreordained, it is worth noting that as late as 1825 important figures in the Exchequer itself could contemplate exactly the reverse – the expansion of the Court's equitable business so 'relieving the Court of Chancery from a portion of its business and thereby giving dispatch to the remainder'.[29]

E. The Handbook

Although the searcher exploring the records of Exchequer's proceedings in equity does not have to wrestle with the same massive accumulation of materials as survive for Chancery, many of the same roadblocks confront her/him. First, there is no 'union' catalogue of parties, places or subjects. Second, the materials for suits are not filed together, but disparately among the 35 'series' (hitherto 'classes') of the records in which the Court's proceedings in equity are at present organized – series whose origins reflect the type of document in question (and/or the office of the Court charged with a given type of document's making or receipt).[30] Thus,

25 Bryson, p. 161.

26 The reporter Edmund Daniel saw the Act of 57 George III c. 18 as one by which, in effect, 'a new Court virtually was created'. Edmund Robert Daniel, *Report of Cases . . . on the Equity Side of the Court of Exchequer* (1834), preface.

27 For such suits, see Chapter Two.

28 For tithe litigation and its decline, see Chapter Two.

29 Unsigned comments of January 1825 submitted to James Elderton (an examiner in the Exchequer) with respect to a proposal for a revision of Exchequer administration; E 167/82 comments on a draft private letter of King's Remembrancer H.W. Vincent to Secretary to the Treasury J.C. Harries, sent Feb. 1825. See also *Hints of the Pending Scheme for Relieving the Suitors in Courts of Equity* (1830); George Price, *A Treatise on the Law of the Exchequer* (1830), preface.

30 In addition to these 35, 106 and C 121 and J 90 contain some exhibits submitted in Exchequer; see below, Chapter Three.

Exchequer equity process and associated records

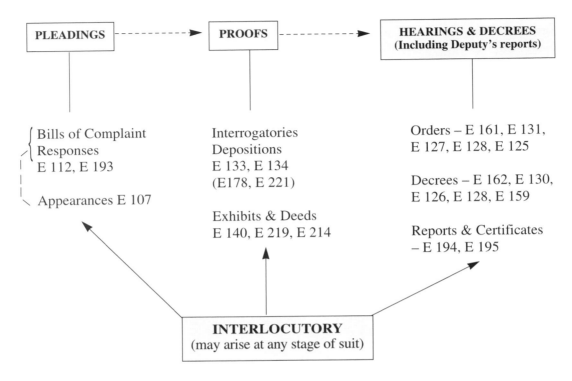

pleadings (bills of complaint, answers, and subsequent replies and counter-replies) are to be found in various pleading series (especially E 112), depositions in other series depending on whether taken in the metropolis or in the provinces (E 133 and E 134), minutes of court proceedings and court orders and decrees in still other series (E 161–62, E 125–28, E 130–31), and so on. And to complicate matters further, neither adequate calendars nor modern indexes exist for most of the principal series.

These problems go far to explain the relative neglect of Exchequer equity records and also explain the decision to prepare a handbook for these materials to parallel my *Chancery Equity Records and Proceedings 1600–1800* (Public Record Office Handbook No 27, 2nd edn. 1998). The basic underpinnings of this handbook are provided by four samples of suits (pleadings) taken from the years 1685, 1735, 1785, and 1819 (years selected, in part, to parallel the samples of pleadings drawn upon in the Chancery handbook), and chosen to mirror the geographical origins of the total number of cases initiated in the Court. Systematic examination of the pleadings in these cases yields valuable information on the subject matter in dispute, the social standing and/or occupation of the litigants, and the gender of the litigants. Furthermore, of the 600 suits in these four sample sets, 300 (the suits from 1685 and 1819) have been fully traced through all the relevant Exchequer classes, thus serving as the bases for descriptions of litigation procedure and for computations such as the average duration of suits. All 600 suits, in turn, are calendared in volume 278 of the List and Index Society (2000).

In addition to the four chronological sample sets, the pleadings for some 260 additional suits emanating from London and Middlesex for the years 1685 and 1785 have been read and tabulated, a task facilitated by the organization of the pleadings by county of origin and by the PRO's production of the pleadings in sizeable portfolios also organized by county.[31] These 260 sets of pleadings, together with the 85 London and Middlesex pleadings of 1685 and 1785 that have been included in the samples for those years, constitute then a second type of selection, i.e., *all* extant London and Middlesex pleadings for those two years. Specific attention has been given to these suits since depositions from metropolitan suits are much less fully listed in the existing finding aids than are those from provincial suits; moreover, it would appear that cases emanating from the metropolis (a growing proportion of the total) displayed a rather different subject profile from those emanating from the provinces. These 345 London and Middlesex sets of pleadings are calendared in volume 35 (2000) of the London Record Society.

Finally, the Handbook also on occasion draws on the analysis of some 258 suits from the mid-1690s, all of which reached advanced stages of process. A detailed account of these suits (and their selection) will be found in Henry Horwitz, 'Chancery's "Younger Sister": the Court of Exchequer and its Equity Jurisdiction, 1629–1841', *Historical Research 72* (June 1999), 160–82. Here they are drawn upon to amplify (and sometimes to qualify) generalizations derived from analysis of the four chronological samples, as well as from the two London and Middlesex sets of cases, and to furnish some of the materials for the specimen searches laid out in Chapter Four of this volume.

The handbook itself is organized in four chapters. The first discusses how the Court did its business, and describes the work of the various officials and offices of the Court. The second examines the range and scope of Exchequer's equity jurisdiction and analyses the character (and origins) of the litigants who came before the Court. The third provides an annotated listing of the relevant Exchequer series and the existing finding aids to those series. The final chapter consists of a number of specimen searches, intended to illustrate in step-by-step fashion how searchers may be able to locate specific information or types of documents among the extant records of Exchequer equity proceedings.

The text is supplemented by a glossary, a bibliography, three appendixes, and an index of persons and subjects.

---

31 For the PRO's present organization of the Exchequer pleadings, see Chapters Two and Three.

CHAPTER ONE
How the Court of Exchequer Conducted Equity Suits

A. Introduction

By the early seventeenth century, on the verge of Exchequer's assumption of a general jurisdiction in equity, the Court of Chancery had evolved into one of the leading royal central courts for the resolution of a wide range of disputes between subjects – coequal, and sometimes more, with the older central common law courts of King's Bench and Common Pleas. Indeed, over the past quarter of a millennium, what had begun as an *ad hoc* system of referral to the Lord Chancellor by the King's Council for the sorting out of civil disputes in an equitable fashion – unconstrained by the rules and norms of common law practice – had evolved into a complex institution with its own distinctive process ('English bill' procedure) and remedies.

By 1603, the contrast between common law and English bill process in Chancery and other central courts using similar methods can be summed up as follows.

First, whereas a civil suit at common law was usually begun with the purchase of a specific writ in *Latin* allowing the litigant to initiate a particular type of action (e.g., an action in debt), a case in Chancery was begun with the submission by the plaintiff of a bill of complaint in *English* detailing in non-technical language his/her situation and asking for relief in general terms.[1] More or less simultaneously, the complainant in Chancery would secure the dispatch of a subpoena ordering the defendant(s) to appear and to answer under oath the bill of complaint. The bill and the defendant's answer, along with any further statements of their cases by the parties, are known collectively as 'the pleadings', and the employment of the vernacular in this and subsequent stages of the suit led contemporaries to employ the term 'English bill' process to characterize not only Chancery procedure but also that of analogous jurisdictions. Thus, the complainant in Chancery was not required to choose a specific form of action (each with its own rules about pleading) from among a range of hundreds of possibilities in the registers of common law writs.

Secondly, one form of intermediate or 'interlocutory' relief that the Court of Chancery could provide, and that was not available at common law, was the injunction. The injunction was an order of the Court barring the defendant either from continuing an ongoing action in another court over the matter raised by the complainant in Chancery (the so-called 'common injunction') or, alternatively, from engaging in any action that might be irremediably damaging to the complainant (the 'special injunction', e.g., to bar the committing of waste on a tenement in which the plaintiff claimed an interest). The interlocutory injunction would remain in force until the defendant had appeared and answered, or in some circumstances, until the controversy was heard by the Court.[2]

---

1 Note, however, that during the later fifteenth and the sixteenth centuries, the Court of King's Bench 'developed its own bill system', partly in competition with Chancery; John H. Baker, *An Introduction to English Legal History* (3rd edn., 1990, hereafter cited as Baker, *Introduction*), pp. 48, 49.
2 Requests for injunctions were commonly made in the bill of complaint. Injunctions were allowed as a matter of course, until the defendant answered, if the defendant was answering by commission in the country. (Interlocutory injunctions should be distinguished from permanent injunctions occasionally issued as part of the Court's judgement.)

Thirdly, whereas the proofs in an early modern civil suit at common law which went to trial consisted of the testimony and cross-examination of each side's witnesses before a jury (for the most part not recorded in writing), the proofs in a contemporaneous Chancery case generally consisted of the statements of witnesses whose depositions were taken out-of-court by either officials or commissioned agents of the Court and recorded in writing for subsequent use.[3] Consequently, the evidence involved in a Chancery suit (or other equity suit) is much more likely to survive than the 'evidence' in a common law suit.[4] Witnesses in and around London were deposed by staff of the Examiner's Office; those in the country by specially commissioned individuals (often local officials in the early seventeenth century). Thus, it was possible in equity proceedings to interrogate witnesses from anywhere in England (or Wales) without requiring them to travel long distances. Moreover, whereas the common law would not, save under special circumstances, allow sworn testimony from a party on grounds of the person's interest in the dispute, no such formal constraint operated under English bill procedure. Indeed, since a defendant's answer was submitted under oath, it was possible, though uncommon, to proceed to a hearing, if the complainant so chose, simply on his/her allegations and the answer of the defendant.

Fourthly, it was possible for the Court to refer matters of fact (including the scrutiny of lengthy documents, such as business accounts) to its own official(s), the Masters in Chancery, for factual inquiry or financial computation, thereby allowing an examination in depth of matters that might well have been too complex to be assimilated by a jury at common law. Such references were usually the result of an initial hearing of the case (with counsel presenting their clients' cases).

Finally, the presiding judge of the Court (the Lord Chancellor or the Master of the Rolls though the latter could only hear causes when the Chancellor was not sitting), upon assessment of the evidence submitted by the parties and reviewed in Masters' reports (if any), and after hearing the arguments of their counsel, would render a decision, recorded verbatim in the book of orders. And this decision, preceded by summaries of the substance of the pleadings, depositions of witnesses, and Master's report, might then (upon payment of the requisite fees) be formally written out on parchment and enrolled, giving the 'decretal order' a greater measure of finality. While a losing party could simply seek a rehearing to reverse a 'decretal order', to contest an enrolled decree he/she had to initiate a more formal reconsideration by way of a bill of review.

Chancery's civil jurisdiction was broad, but by no means all-encompassing.[5] Nor is it easy to define its boundaries, save to say that the Court exercised jurisdiction over issues that the common law courts had not been prepared to deal with during the first two centuries of Chancery's evolution. This can be illustrated with respect to disputes over land. In principle,

---

3 It should also be noted that the action of debt (when specialty was lacking) was normally decided by wager at law (that is, oath-helping or compurgation), rather than by testimony before a jury, and that such actions were very frequent at common law up to the early seventeenth century; Baker, *Introduction*, pp. 87–8.

4 Thus, a litigant at common law might initiate a Chancery suit for the purpose of discovery and deposition – in particular, to depose a witness who, by reason of age or expected departure from the realm, might not be present when the litigant's common-law case came before a jury at trial.

5 Horwitz, *Chancery Equity Records*, chap. 2. And see Chapter Two below for a quantitative analysis of the subject matter of disputes coming before Exchequer in equity.

Chancery could not decide *legal* title in land (i.e., title in fee simple or fee tail); by definition, *legal* title had been and remained the province of the common law courts. Yet Chancery might well consider disputes centring on land, if a trust or mortgage were involved or if what was at issue was possession or use rights. In this fashion, what came to be known as *equitable* title, rights to land adjudicated in Chancery, also took shape.[6] Moreover, to enforce its decisions, Chancery could make permanent an injunction against waste or to quiet possession. It could also decree 'specific performance' (i.e., order a party to perform a given act such as to convey title to a piece of land that the party had originally contracted to sell). Insofar, then, as the Court could and did direct the behaviour of the parties with respect to the controversy, it was in a position to compel conduct that at least for the duration of the parties' interests in the property in question came close to resolving a range of land disputes.[7] And to give force to its decisions, it could punish the recalcitrant party by contempt process (imprisonment till she/he conformed) or even sequester that party's property until compliance.[8]

Here it should be observed that the Court of Chancery was only the most important of a number of courts employing variants of English bill procedure in the early seventeenth century. A host of such jurisdictions existed in the provinces, including the 'equity side' of the Councils of the North and of Wales and also more geographically-circumscribed jurisdictions such as the Chancery Court of the county palatine of Durham. While Chancery's position in relation to these jurisdictions was one of 'dominance' as a central court of equity *vis-à-vis* provincial ones, their business in the early 1600s was extensive.[9] At the same time, other central courts using English bill procedure included the Court of Star Chamber and the Court of Requests. Thus at Westminster, too, litigants seeking equitable remedies had a number of choices, although in Star Chamber 'the criminal aspect was more to the fore . . . by Stuart times', while Chancery appears to have valued Requests principally as an 'alternative channel for smaller and trivial litigation' which did not meet its own jurisdictional threshholds (£10 in value or six acres in extent or a tenement yielding at least 40 shillings yearly).[10] And in addition, by the early seventeenth century, the four Barons of the Court of Exchequer had been exercising a jurisdiction in equity for several generations, and employing English bill

---

6 Hence, Chancery's jurisdiction over feoffees to uses and also, later, the evolution of the equity of redemption – the right of a borrower upon mortgage to redeem the property despite an earlier failure to satisfy the terms of the mortgage. See Baker, *Introduction*, pp. 286–7, 355–6.

7 Edith G. Henderson, 'Legal Rights to Land in the Early Chancery', *American Journal of Legal History* 26 (1982), 97–122, points out that many early Chancery decrees concerned land, with the complainant often alleging that he/she was in pursuit of the deeds of title. By the Restoration, the Court had made it a rule that a plaintiff suing for deeds must put in an affidavit swearing she/he was not in fact in possession of them.

8 Similarly, it is often said that Chancery could not order damages – that its particular remedy for a breach of a contract or the like was specific performance. But on occasion, it did impose monetary damages. See Peter McDermott, 'Jurisdiction of the Court of Chancery to Award Damages', *Law Quarterly Review* 108 (1992), 652–73.

9 W. J. Jones, 'Palatine performance in the seventeenth century', in *The English Commonwealth 1547–1640* (1979), ed. Peter Clark *et al.*, 189–204.

10 Baker, *Introduction,* p. 137; William. J. Jones, *The Elizabethan Court of Chancery* (1967), p. 382. Requests, to be sure, was not simply a poor man's Court, and in any case Chancery did admit an occasional litigant *in forma pauperis* – that is, providing legal assistance and waiving fees. See also Tim Stretton, *Women Waging Law in Elizabethan England* (1998). For such proceedings in Exchequer, see below, Chapter Four.

procedure in much the the same fashion as Chancery did even though, as we have seen, theirs was still in 1603 a jurisdiction available only to a limited set of classes of parties.

In turn, when, under the troubled circumstances of the later 1640s and early 1650s, the Barons of the Exchequer ceased to enforce the requirement that suitors in equitable causes initiated before them have a direct connection with the royal revenue, the Court took on a similar range of litigants and of disputes. To be sure, not all was identical as between Chancery and Exchequer, and indeed one of the questions we will have to consider in Chapter Two is why a given suitor might prefer to pursue his cause in the one court rather than the other. Here, however, our concern is primarily to sketch the ways in which complainants pursued their causes in the Exchequer, a topic characterized by many similarities between the two courts but also marked by some significant differences.

B. The Conduct of Equitable Proceedings in the Court of Exchequer

In broad terms, the conduct of equitable proceedings in Chancery and Exchequer can be viewed from two different, if overlapping perspectives. The first is that of the litigant – especially the complainant who initiated the suit. Basically, the complainant was seeking some form of assistance from the court. Ostensibly, and often in fact, that was the remedying of a wrong done to him/her. However, the litigant might have other aims in view as well.

Among the more common objectives of complainants in equity, in addition to the righting of a wrong, were:

(1) securing the court's formal sanction for a course of action upon which the parties were already agreed (i.e., a collusive proceeding, most often encountered in the administration of a trust or estate);

(2) putting pressure upon an opponent to compromise or to settle a dispute by the threat of expense and delay involved in judicial proceedings;

(3) blocking – at least for a time – adverse action in another court;

(4) using judicial process as a means of making one's opponent disclose his/her own position or situation by putting him/her under a compulsion to file an answer under oath; and /or

(5) securing discovery via the taking of depositions to preserve testimony (i.e., of an aged or sick individual or of a person leaving the country) to be used either in the immediate proceedings or in litigation in other courts.

From a somewhat different perspective, it could be said that a complainant was seeking either (a) some kind of formal action from the court (whether a binding judgement or an interlocutory remedy (the injunction), *or* (b) some kind of leverage against an opponent which did not require any definitive decision from the court. And here it should be noted that the worst that could happen to a complainant was to have her/his bill formally dismissed (a dismission); the Court would not actually issue a decree against her/him.[11]

---

11 However, see the discussion below at p. 22 of cross bills.

As complainants came into court with diverse aims, so the courts and their officials also had a variety of concerns. For one thing, the various officers had their own material interests to serve. Most of the subordinate officials of Exchequer, as those of other courts, depended on the fee income derived from the performance of their functions (a common feature of governmental administration of the era).[12]

In broad terms, the personnel of the equity side of the Exchequer as it developed from the sixteenth century onwards may be subdivided into judicial officers and clerical officers.[13] The judges of the equity jurisdiction of the Exchequer were, in form, headed by the Treasurer and the Chancellor of the Exchequer, but in fact the former rarely acted in a judicial capacity, while the latter did so only infrequently (usually for the purpose of breaking a tie between the equally-divided four Barons). It was the Barons, then, who normally presided, sitting as a group of four judges up to the 'reforms' of 1817.[14]

The clerical officers were headed by the King's Remembrancer, though in fact this office became a sinecure (held by various members of the Fanshawe family for much of the period from 1565 to 1716) and the work of this office was performed by deputy from 1616 to 1823.[15] However, it was not until the tenure as Deputy of Tobias Eden between 1672 and 1698 that the Deputyship achieved its full importance, with Eden taking over from the Barons the business of taxing court costs of the parties and from the Auditors of the Land Revenue the responsibility of investigating questions of fact referred to them by the Barons (so-called 'references') and preparing reports thereon. However, the balance of responsibility between the Deputy and other clerical officers remained to some degree unstable. Thus, for instance while Eden's successor as Deputy, Robert Barker, took on the responsibility for the examination of witnesses, his successors in the eighteenth century largely left it to the clerks in court (the eight sworn clerks and the twenty-four 'under' or side clerks) to execute references from the Barons, and the clerks also appear to have made inroads into the taxing of costs and the taking of minutes.[16]

The principal staff under the King's Remembrancer (or in practice, the Deputy Remembrancer) were the sworn clerks – the Exchequer counterparts of the six clerks in Chancery.[17] Each litigant was required to employ one of the eight sworn clerks, nominally to be his/her 'attorney', in practice to handle the paperwork of their cases. In turn, the bulk of that paperwork was actually the business of the subordinates of the sworn clerks, the twenty-four side clerks (from whom, when a vacancy occurred, the sworn clerks themselves were chosen

---

12 For quarrels among the clerks at court over the division of fee income, see fn. 19 below.

13 The following section on personnel is a summary of Bryson, pp. 75–8 and 65–6, as amended and supplemented by R. M. Ball, 'Tobias Eden, Change and Conflict in the Exchequer Office, 1672–1698', *Journal of Legal History* XI (1990), 70–89.

14 For a discussion of the change wrought by Parliament in 1817 and its impact, see above, p. 7.

15 For fluctuations in the importance of the Deputy Remembrancer in the administration of the Exchequer Office, see R. M. Ball, 'The King's Remembrancer's Office in the Eighteenth Century', *Journal of Legal History* XI (1990), 90–113.

16 Ball, 'Eden', p. 85; Ball, 'King's Remembrancer', pp. 91–2.

17 The senior sworn clerk held the office of first secondary; he had the duty of administering the oaths of office and the custody of various books and documents. The next senior sworn clerk was given the office of second secondary which involved no responsibilities other than the keeping of certain books. Hence, the eight sworn clerks are sometimes referred to as the two secondaries and the six sworn clerks.

by the King's Remembrancer acting at his discretion).[18]

Each sworn clerk had the right to appoint three side clerks, with each appointee to be apprenticed for a term of five years. After completion of that apprenticeship, the services, attendances, and fees of the side clerks were the same as those of the sworn clerks, save that they did not administer oaths nor read documents in court. Even so, being in form at least the servants of their respective sworn clerks (who often styled them in the seventeenth century their 'under clerks'), the side clerks put their respective sworn clerks' names onto the documents of the cases which they handled.[19]

The duties of the sworn and side clerks (collectively styled the clerks in court during the eighteenth century) on the equity side of Exchequer were to issue all writs, to enter, file, copy, and enrol all matters connected with the suits of their clients, to attend the Court at the hearing and read the documents and depositions, to attend the Deputy Remembrancer on references, to draw up decrees and orders, and to procure all necessary signatures. They were also responsible under the Deputy Remembrancer for the keeping of the records of the Court. Moreover, though not solicitors and only occasionally barristers, they remained 'occupied as lawyers' in equity business by providing overall direction of the suit and a specialised knowlege of the procedures of the Court and especially the practice of the Office.[20] The clerks in court, along with the Deputy Remembrancer, were expected to attend the Court when it sat and otherwise 'constantly' attend at the Exchequer Office in term time. The clerks' hours were reported in 1798 to be from 9 a.m. until dark, and from the beginning of Michaelmas and Hilary terms until the conclusion of the sitting of the Court after those terms 'respectively until 9 o'clock at night.'[21]

Besides these clerical officials, the King's Remembrancer (or his deputy) was assisted by a clerk, and under each Baron was an examiner (for taking depositions in the metropolis) and a clerk. In addition, during the seventeenth century, the Deputy Remembrancer had two other personal clerks who performed the tasks of taking of the minutes of decrees and orders and of entering them in the appropriate records. However, in the eighteenth century this function was performed by the Deputy Remembrancer, or in his absence by one of the sworn clerks.

The early nineteenth century also witnessed potentially significant changes in the implementation of the duties of the King's Remembrancer. An Act of Parliament in 1820 (1 George IV c. 35) instituted two additional posts to handle the work of the Remembrancer, hitherto largely the responsibility of his deputy. The posts were two Masterships, one to attend

18 For instructions issued by the sworn clerks to the 'under clerks' in 1649, suggestive of various sins of commission and omission in the performance of their clerical tasks – i.a., misfiling, unauthorized removal of documents from the Office, unauthorized making of copies (thus depriving the sworn clerks of their fees), and counterfeiting of the keys to the record rooms at Westminster – see E 164/6, ff. 88–9.

19 As in Chancery, so these two orders of clerks in Exchequer could differ sharply over the division of fee income, with sometimes highly detrimental effects on the performance of their duties (e.g., the failure of the Sworn Clerks between Michaelmas 1673 and Hilary 1675 to enter decrees in the entering books); Ball, 'Eden', p. 81. See also H. Horwitz, 'Record-keepers in the Court of Chancery and their "Record" of Accomplishment in the Seventeenth and Eighteenth Centuries', *Historical Research* 70 (1997), 34–51.

20 Ball, 'King's Remembrancer', p. 98. However, most of the drafting of pleadings would seem to have been carried out by counsel; p. 100.

21 E 167/77, 'an account of the Office of his Majesty's Remembrancer in the Court of Exchequer', draft of 16 March 1798 prepared for submission to the House of Commons.

in court and take the minutes of orders and decrees, as well as to handle references, the other (also designated as Accountant General) to be responsible for the safekeeping and investment of all monies paid into court. These new officers were to be independent of the authority of the King's Remembrancer, while in turn the post of clerk of the reports was created to act as a check upon the new Accountant General.[22] However, these new posts, along with most others involving the performance of responsibilities in the equity jurisdiction, were abolished in 1841 when the jurisdiction itself came to an end.

This array of Exchequer officials entrusted with duties in the Court's equitable business (and often also having other responsibilities in Exchequer business) carried out their work in two principal locations. One was the so-called Exchequer Office located at the north-west corner of King's Bench Walk in the Inner Temple. This was built during the Interregnum by the then King's Remembrancer, the second Viscount Fanshawe, to replace an earlier, and less convenient, office in Warwick Lane near St Paul's, but the new office itself had to be reconstructed after the Great Fire of 1666. Thereafter, the Inner Temple site would remain the principal location for the transaction of the administrative business of the Court.[23] However, there was no attempt made to transfer to the Exchequer Office the substantial volume of existing Court records.[24] Rather, they remained stored in various existing Exchequer sites in Westminster Hall, with periodic transfers of additional records being made to those ill-suited quarters from the Exchequer Office.

Throughout, the four Barons continued to sit in Westminster Hall, at least during term time, to hear equity suits and to transact their other judicial business. The Court sat in a building attached to the western wall of Westminster Hall at the northern end, reached through the north door of Westminster Hall, and then up a staircase immediately on the right. There was situated both a large court room (the Exchequer Chamber) and a smaller one (variously known as the Inner Court of the Exchequer or the Little Exchequer Court).[25] In term time, the Exchequer did equity business daily (Monday through Saturday).[26]

The result of the distance between these two sites was some inconvenience for both Court officials and suitors; Westminster Hall was nearly one and a quarter miles away from the Temple. However, out of term, the Barons sat closer to the Exchequer Office, sometimes at Gray's Inn and also on occasion at Serjeants' Inn.[27]

As the physical separation of the Court from its principal office was an inconvenient

22 Previously the Deputy Remembrancer had often been referred to as the 'Master' by analogy to the Masters of Chancery.

23 Ball, 'Eden', p. 70. We may well ponder whether it was simply a coincidence that the move of the Exchequer Office to a location more convenient to suitors came in the same years that the Court began to tolerate, perhaps even to welcome, suitors who were not privileged persons in the traditional senses.

24 For the decay and depredations suffered by the Court's records in the eighteenth and early nineteenth centuries, see in general Bryson, pp. 82–6.

25 The Exchequer Chamber was also the site of hearings on writs of error from any of the central common law courts.

26 According to Kirkby's account, on Mondays and Thursdays the Court heard causes only; on Tuesdays and Fridays, motions and causes; on Wednesdays motions, exceptions, pleas and demurrers; and on Saturdays motions only. William Kirkby, *Rules and Orders of the Court of Exchequer, Relative to the Practice of the King's Remembrancer's Office* (1794), p. 124. For the revised schedule from 1817 onwards, see George Price, *Report of Cases . . . in the Court of Exchequer*, IV (1819), 21–2.

27 According to Kirkby, a week or ten days after term, the Barons sat in Serjeants' Inn Hall to hear causes and motions (save after Easter term). This was after the Chief Baron sat at the London and Middlesex *nisi prius* sessions. Kirkby, p. 124.

fact of life for both officials and suitors (though paralleling the Court of Chancery's layout), so the Court's operation was considerably influenced by two other rather contradictory concerns. One was the commitment in principle of the Barons, as judges in equity, to get to the bottom of the individual complaints brought before the Court in order to render appropriate relief, and especially in cases where fraud might have been committed.[28] As one learned student of equitable practice has observed: by contrast to common law, 'the first object of inquiry in Equity is the defendant's conscience, rather than the plaintiff's right'.[29] The other was the pressure to deal with the rising tide of cases that washed over the central courts in the later sixteenth century and much of the seventeenth century.[30]

All in all, then, the way in which the Court and its officials handled the cases that came before them was a mixture of genuine enquiry and bureaucratic self-interest, compounded by overwork and complicated by the manoeuvres of the opposing parties for whom delay and obfuscation might well be advantageous.

These intersecting concerns and perspectives can, in turn, be discerned in the formal orders of the Court, in the ways litigants behaved, and in the channels through which their suits progressed. The earliest recorded orders of Exchequer regulating the conduct of proceedings in equity date from the 1620s, with a fuller set of rules promulgated some time between June 1658 and January 1660 and issued under the imprimatur of the then four Barons. In turn, various versions of these rules, with additions, were published in the course of the later seventeenth and the eighteenth centuries.[31] How far these rules reflected current practice by then is at best a moot point. Certainly, it appears that by the eighteenth century some rules of Court were more honoured in the breach than in the observance, reflecting the informal supersession in current practice of older standards.[32] Yet newer ways were not always embodied in orders of Court, thus further complicating the solicitor's task in managing suits (while helping to assist the clerks in court to maintain their predominance). As Lord Chancellor Eldon remarked in an 1813 Chancery case: 'Much of the modern practice will, I fear, be found inconsistent with subsisting orders, without any contradiction of them by subsequent orders; and, upon principle, repeated decisions, forming a series of practice, as it must be, against an order, may with safety be taken to amount to a reversal of that order.'[33]

---

28 See Chief Baron Pengelly's biographer's observation contrasting the Barons' role in law with that in equity: 'His administration in the *Exchequer* exactly suited the nature of that Court; he fully explain'd the Law whenever Causes were try'd before a Jury, and decided impartially in Equity, where it remain'd in the Breast of the Court solely to determine.' Philalethes, *Some Private Passages of the Life of Sir Thomas Pengelly* (1733), p. 28. I owe this reference to Professor De Lloyd Guth.

29 *Lord Nottingham's 'Manual of Chancery Practice' and 'Prolegomena of Chancery and Equity'*, ed. D. E. C. Yale (1965), p. 23.

30 For trends in litigation, see C. W. Brooks, 'Litigation and Society in England, 1200–1996' in his *Lawyers, Litigation and English Society since 1450* (1998), esp. pp. 66–73.

31 Bryson, pp. 197–9, a full listing of locations of lists of rules of the Court of the Exchequer. The 1658–60 set contains 50 separate rules; the 1687 set, also promulgated by the Barons, contains 58 rules; and between 1687 and Kirkby's compilation in 1794 some 45 more were promulgated (of which only 31 are listed in Kirkby).

32 See, for example, the Court's acknowledgment that its rule of 19 James I governing the issue of subpoenas had long since been superseded in practice so that it must 'at this day be considered obsolete'. Taylor v. Riley (1821), *The English Reports*, vol. 147, 146–7 (Price, IX, 388).

33 In Boehm v. De Tastet (1813), quoted in Joseph Parkes, *A History of the Court of Chancery* (1828), p. 451.

As the Court's concerns and conduct were articulated in its orders and then modified over time by shifting patterns of observance, so complainants' diverse aims and objectives were mirrored in the conduct of their suits. It is, indeed, noteworthy that many complainants did not pursue their suits very far. For over two-fifths of the sample suits for the period (252 of 600), there survive only the bills of complaint, and in most of these instances there is no evidence that an answer was ever made.[34] So we must presume that for a sizeable minority of complainants, filing of the bill (or even the securing of a subpoena ordering their opponents to answer an as-yet unfiled bill) sufficed to promote an informal settlement or otherwise exhausted their commitment to action in court.[35]

For the majority of suitors who did pursue their cases further, there were significant costs. Not only did they have to pay fees to Court officials for the performance of their functions, but there were also the expenses incurred in employing their own legal representatives.[36]

In dissecting the course of an equity suit in Exchequer, two other general features need to be kept in mind. In the first place, as it was the complainant who took the initiative at the outset, so thereafter it was the respective parties who largely determined the pace at which the suit proceeded. The Court had rules and deadlines, but it was up to the parties or their representatives to see to their observance. For example, it was up to the defendant to move for the dismissal of a suit if a plaintiff had failed to respond to the defendant's answer within the requisite time and it was also up to the defendant to make counter-arguments if under such circumstances a plaintiff came into Court, sought to excuse his previous failure to act, and moved to keep the suit alive.

Secondly, in pursuing their courses of action, the parties had to manoeuvre within the framework of the Court's bureaucratic structure, with the additional handicap of having to pursue clerical business at the Exchequer Office at the Temple and judicial business in (for the most part) Westminster Hall. The parties, or their representatives, had also to bear in mind the Court's calendar. However, during term the Barons did hear equity causes every weekday.[37]

Like the common law courts, Exchequer equity observed four terms – Michaelmas (in the later autumn), Hilary (early in the New Year), Easter, and Trinity (late in the spring) – and entries in the minute and order books were grouped by term. Moreover, unlike the Lord

---

34 The comparable proportion for the Chancery sample suits is less than one-quarter (174 of 729).

35 It was possible for a potential complainant in Exchequer (or Chancery) to secure the delivery of a subpoena to a potential defendant before the complainant filed his bill; but costs would attach and his suit would be disallowed if he failed to file within four days after the defendant did appear. There was frequent criticism of this aspect of English bill process as allowing the unscrupulous to harass their enemies, not least because the subpoena did not specify what was at issue in the suit. However, one Interregnum defender of Chancery – noting that 'in this last year' some 9,000 subpoenas to answer had been issued but only 6,000 bills of complaint exhibited in that court – read this as evidence that the delivery of a subpoena often sufficed to promote out-of-court settlements: *A View of the Regulation of the Chancery* (1654), p. 2. The practice of early delivery of subpoenas in suits in the central courts of equity was abolished by statute in 1706 but it survived this legislative ban.

36 For a detailed and term by term breakdown of the Court and legal costs that various types of suits might entail by the later 1700s, see Appendix One. Charles Turner, an early eighteenth-century solicitor, left behind detailed records of charges and fees in two Exchequer suits of the 1720s (records later put in evidence in a Chancery case); C 107/123, ff. 11 and 254–9. For varying comparisons of Exchequer and Chancery costs offered by the witnesses to the Lords' inquiry of 1840, see *JHL* 72 (questions 225–8, 641–77, 783, 796).

37 Charles Barton, *An Historical Treatise of a Suit in Equity* (1796), p. 186 note.

Chancellor and the Master of the Rolls, the four Barons of the Exchequer went on assizes through the kingdom twice yearly, during the interval between Hilary and Easter terms and during the long vacation in July and August.

What, then, were the stages of an Exchequer equity suit from the filing of a bill of complaint to the formal hearing of the cause? The account that follows is based on two principal sources: (1) the practice manuals (listed in the Bibliography) published for the use of would-be practitioners in Exchequer (and the other central courts); and (2) the evidence that has been accumulated from tracing over 500 Exchequer equity suits, the majority from the later seventeenth century and the remainder from the early nineteenth century. On the one hand, the practice manuals are informative about the technical requirements parties had to satisfy (though their accuracy has to be tested against direct evidence of Court practice).[38] On the other hand, the traced cases indicate, in a way that goes beyond the technical descriptions of the manuals, how parties to those particular suits actually proceeded, and their findings may on occasion be supplemented by extant printed reports of Exchequer equity cases.[39]

C. The Procedure of the Court: the Practice Manuals

The first published manual dealing with the judicial activities of the Court of Exchequer, Peter Osborne's *The Practice of the Exchequer Court,* appeared in print in 1658, in the decade in which the Court assumed a general equity jurisdiction. And while Osborne's work sheds no light on this development (since in fact it was written in 1572), rather more enlightening is an essay (dating from the 1630s) entitled 'Of English Bills and the proceedings thereupon in the Exchequer' appearing as an appendix to Osborne.[40]

'Of English Bills' was later either extracted or reprinted by more comprehensive manuals including Sir William Booth's *The Compleat Solicitor* (1666, and subsequent editions), *The Practick Part of the Law* (from the 1676 edition onwards up to the last of 1724), William Bohun's *The Practising Attorney* (1724, followed by three more editions up to 1737), and *The Compleat Clerk in Court* (1726). Also appearing several times was *A Compendium of the Several Branches of Practice in the Court of Exchequer* (1688) which was compiled by William Brown. It consists of a short essay by William Byrde (probably dating to 1615 or shortly thereafter) entitled 'A Discourse of the Court of the Exchequer' and focusing chiefly on the revenue jurisdiction of the Court, followed by an extensive collection of forms and

---

38 For a warning note about the accuracy of early nineteenth century manuals of practice sounded by one Chancery clerk in court, see *Parliamentary Papers* 1826 (143) xvi, app. B(24) 552. See also Fowler, I, 64: 'It is not very accurately ascertained in the books of practice, or in the reports, in what cases a suit becomes defective without being absolutely abated. . .'

39 For bibliography of these printed reports, see Bryson, pp. 199–201.

40 Authorship and dating of Osborne's work were established by R. B. Outhwaite, 'Note on *The Practice of the Exchequer Court, With its several Offices and Officers*; by Sir T. F.,' *English Historical Review* 81 (1966), 337–9. The appendix to Osborne (a copy of which is to be found at E 369/118, ff. 148–57) should be distinguished from the somewhat later 'Orders and rules of proceedings' in the Exchequer (a copy of which is to be found at E 163/19/17, ff. 7–19) which was promulgated by the then Barons in the closing years of the Interregnum. Nonetheless, there is a considerable overlap between the two documents.

examples illustrating all aspects of Exchequer's judicial business.[41] In turn, the *Compendium* was reprinted in 1699 and 1725 under the title *The Practice of the Court of Exchequer at Westminster.*

As was the case with respect to most other central courts, the late eighteenth century saw a new burst of publications, with each of the three concerned with Exchequer equity much more detailed in exposition than any of the earlier works. Most important was the two-volume work of David Burton Fowler (himself a sworn clerk of the Court): his *The Practice of the Court of Exchequer upon Proceedings in Equity* was first published in 1795, and reissued in 1817. In 1796 Charles Barton published *An Historical Treatise of a Suit in Equity* in which the young barrister in a single volume presented a work covering both Chancery and Exchequer, while remarking on their occasional differences. Finally, one may mention Samuel Turner's 1806 work, *An epitome of the practice of the equity side of the Court of Exchequer*, mainly notable for the wealth of forms the author provides, along with many one-sentence digests of cases by subject. In addition, it is relevant to note that Fowler, Barton and Turner all drew extensively on John Freeman Mitford's *Treatise on the Pleadings in Suits in the Court of Chancery by English Bill* (1780), thus again illustrating the substantial overlap between Chancery and Exchequer practice.

As the quantity of evidence provided by the Exchequer equity practice manuals considerably improves with the passage of time, so there is, in fact, no comparison in range and depth of treatment between the reference materials available in the later seventeenth and early eighteenth centuries and those newly available one hundred years or so later. Thus, these earlier works and collections, however informative and valuable, can at best provide only part of the picture for the first century of the Exchequer's general jurisdiction in equity. Consequently, in the discussion that follows, which tracks Bryson's analysis, Fowler's account is taken to be authoritative even for the seventeenth century unless there is positive evidence to the contrary.

(I) The First Stage: Pleadings

The initial stage of an Exchequer equity suit was the filing of a written bill of complaint on (stamped) parchment.[42] In principle, bills were supposed to follow a standard tripartite format:

(1) the complainant gave his/her name, status and/or occupation, and place of residence;
(2) stated the relevant facts of his/her complaint, and
(3) went on to allege that it was impossible to secure a remedy without the Court's action and so prayed relief – relief which normally included a request for a subpoena and often also a request for an injunction.

41 For the dating of Byrde, see W. H. Bryson, 'Exchequer Equity Bibliography', *American Journal of Legal History* 14 (1970), 341–3.

42 The stamp, instituted under the Stamp Act of 1694, was a record of the payment of stamp duty. Bills filed by the Attorney-General were technically known as 'English informations', but they differed from 'English bills' only 'in their style'. Most of the bills filed by the Attorney-General did not immediately concern the rights of the Crown but rather the public interest in some more general and diffuse sense (e.g., the operation of a charity); in such English informations the parties moving the Attorney-General to action are named as 'relators' and are considered liable for costs and the Attorney-General is said to be proceeding *ex. rel.* Fowler, I, 117–18.

By the later eighteenth century, this relatively simple format had been elaborated, but the crux of the matter remained the statement of the facts of the complaint. Of the nine parts of a bill distinguished by Fowler, perhaps the only one worthy of additional remark is the standard allegation of confederacy between the named defendant(s) and unnamed parties. If this formula had any specific function (which Fowler denied), it was to allow for the subsequent inclusion of additional defendants to the case.[43] The bill was unsworn but it had to be signed by the complainant's counsel. His signature attested to his belief that the complainant was not acting frivolously or without cause.

The bill was filed in the Exchequer Office under the supervision of one of the clerks in court. That individual clerk was thereafter responsible for the paperwork in the case (though the clerks' role as attorneys to the litigant was increasingly supplemented by the parties' employment of their own 'solicitors' to look after their cases in Exchequer).[44] In filing the bill, the clerk was supposed to endorse the term and the regnal year of the submission of the bill on the top left-hand corner of the document.[45] Beneath this endorsement would be written the county of origin of the suit, the number of the bill for that particular county and reign (corresponding to the number of the bill entered in the bill book), and the last name or initial of the sworn clerk representing the plaintiff (either himself or via one of his side clerks). At the foot was entered the order for process in the suit, the *fiat*, which was signed by one of the Barons of the Court – a necessary preliminary, in theory, to the issue of a subpoena.[46]

Once a bill of complaint was filed, the next issue was getting the defendant to appear (i.e., to acknowledge the Court's jurisdiction) and to make a response, again in writing.[47] Several different kinds of responses might be offered, in addition or in alternative to the usual one, the sworn answer.[48] One alternative, the disclaimer, was aimed at taking the defendant wholly out of the suit by disavowing any interest in the matter in dispute and ceding any claim that he/she might be thought to have in the matter to the complainant. A second, the demurrer, sought to evade the force of the complaint by admitting the truth of the complainant's factual allegations but then going on to argue that they did not present any cause for which the defendant might reasonably be expected to answer. A third, the plea, amounted to the raising of a ground in law, frequently jurisdictional in nature, to forestall the complainant – e.g., that

---

43 Fowler, I, 28–38. See also C. Churches, '"Equity against a purchaser shall not be": a seventeenth-century case study in landholding and indebtedness', *Parergon* new series 11, no. 2 (Dec. 1993), p. 78 (speaking of the allegation of confederacy in a Chancery bill of complaint: the complainant 'very well knew there was no such confederacy'; his purpose was to secure 'from the other parties their assurance that their claims [against the principal defendant] had been met in full or else of what remained outstanding, the whole to be put on record in the court.')

44 At the same time, because of the decline of business, for much of the eighteenth century the staff was at less than full strength, falling to as low as fifteen in the mid-century decades. Ball, 'King's Remembrancer', p. 93.

45 In our samples and selections of bills, month and day were included in about one-third of later 17th century cases, virtually none of the later 18th century cases, and perhaps two-fifths of the early 19th century cases. Sometimes month and day were provided by the entering clerk; on other occasions, the Baron signifying the Court's assent to the issuance of the subpoena dated his signature to the *fiat*.

46 Bryson, pp. 109–10.

47 See below, pp. 23, 30, 60, for a discussion of 'appearance'. It certainly did not always mean that the appearing defendant answered (or vice versa).

48 Sir William Holdsworth, *A History of English Law* IX (1926), has a full and informative discussion of pleading at 376–408, including examples of bills and an answer.

the matter in question was not one of equity and hence not to be heard in Exchequer but in some other court, usually either a court of common law or an ecclesiastical court or, alternatively, that the complainant was barred from suing by some specific disability (e.g., prior outlawry). However, unlike answers, none of these alternative forms of response was regarded as attesting to matters of fact. And since none was regarded as having the weight of evidence, it was not held to be necessary that the respondent swear to their truth.[49]

Such alternate 'answers' were normally heard and passed upon by the Barons themselves (by contrast to the situation in Chancery where demurrers, pleas and disclaimers were normally referred to a Master or to the common law judges for a recommendation as to acceptance or rejection).[50] Should a demurrer or a plea be rejected by the Court, the defendant would have to submit an answer. Defendants might choose at the outset to respond in the alternative, submitting simultaneously, for instance, both a demurrer and an answer. If the demurrer was rejected, the suit would then go forward on the basis of the answer. However, for a defendant less interested in expedition (and perhaps with a bigger purse than the plaintiff's), the opportunity for delay inherent in first offering a plea or demurrer (or even an insufficient answer) may have been significant provided that such a defendant was answering in the Court (not *in absentia* from the country by response delivered to commissioners). To put it slightly differently, since defendants who chose to respond by commission from the country (i.e., if they were ill or dwelt 15 miles or more from London) were given extra time as compared to those who replied in Court, it was thought inappropriate that they should be allowed a 'demurrer or delatory plea' as well.[51]

In turn, a 'sufficient' or unexceptionable answer involved a denial (unless the suit was a collusive one), to be attested under oath by the party, of all or some of the relevant or material factual allegations of the complainant. The denial would commonly go hand in hand with the defendant's own version of the controversy or disputed transaction.

Besides disclaimer, plea, demurrer, or answer, one other additional option was open to some defendants. That was to file a cross bill – to make the complainant the defendant in a separate but inter-linked suit. This was a course the defendant could pursue if he thought the original bill itself (inadvertently) opened the door for a claim by him against the complainant. A cross bill might be filed at any time during the pleadings stage, and thereafter proceedings on the two bills would usually move forward together. Thus, it was possible for a complainant to have his original bill dismissed and judgement found against him on the defendant's cross bill.[52]

Although defendants had a variety of options by way of response to the bill of complaint, it was not always easy to get a named defendant to appear and respond. Hence, the complainant's invocation of the Court's power to subpoena (a writ ordering the recipient to

---

49 The weight of evidence of an answer was such that it took the testimony of two contradictory witnesses to overcome it with respect to any matter of fact alleged therein: Bryson, p. 117.

50 Horwitz, *Chancery Equity Records*, p. 15. Unlike the Lord Chancellor or the Master of the Rolls, the Barons had a common law as well as their equitable jurisdiction.

51 Rule 6, E 163/19/17. It should be noted, however, that disclaimers were in fact rare, and demurrers and pleas very uncommon (in the 1685 sample, three demurrers, two pleas, and one plea filed with a demurrer; in the 1819 sample, three demurrers and one plea filed with an answer).

52 Bryson, p. 126, indicates he found no cross bills in the sixteenth century, but occasional cross bills are encountered in later decades. Only four cross bills have been identified in conjunction with the 1685 and 1819 samples.

appear and to answer, subject to penalty for failure).[53] Subpoenas, as has been noted, were often (though by no means invariably) issued before the actual filing of the bill both in Chancery and Exchequer for the 'ease', according to Thomas Powell, of suitors.[54] Since the usual or 'common' subpoena used to compel appearance and answer failed to state the terms of the plaintiff's bill, defendants faced with a subpoena but no bill could find themselves in a quandary.[55] On the other hand, costs would be assessed by the Court against the plaintiff if he/she failed to file a bill by the time the subpoena was returnable and the suit itself would be dismissed if the plaintiff failed to produce the bill within four days of the defendant's appearance.

Nor is this to suggest that a subpoena alone would induce every defendant to appear, and the Court had more drastic powers of compulsion at its disposal, including the power of attachment (imprisonment or at least the necessity of putting up bail until compliance) and even the power to sequester a defendant's property. But it was not until 1732 that Parliament legislated to provide for the problem of the failure of the defendant in proceedings in equity to appear at all; under that legislation, after public advertisement in *The London Gazette*, courts of equity might proceed *ex parte* and, if need be, render judgement by default.[56] Even so, no small part of the cause of delay in the initial stage of a suit even after 1732 was the Court's reluctance to proceed to judgement without the appearance of and answer by the defendant.[57]

Under most circumstances, a defendant did not need to appear in person; an appearance by his legal representative would suffice. But whether the written answer was submitted in town or to commissioners in the country, it was – unlike the plaintiff's bill – to be made under oath (save in special circumstances), and the defendant was bound by whatever admissions he made therein that were germane to the suit.[58] Answers, in turn, might be backed up by documentation intended to support the defendant's position, and such material – often in the form of schedules of account – would be attached to and filed with the answer itself.[59]

With the defendant appearing and answering, the stage was set for further exchanges between the parties. On the one hand, the complainant might, provided he acted within four days after the answer was filed, offer exceptions to the answer itself, on the grounds that it contained scandalous matter or, more commonly, that it was 'insufficient', i.e., that it did not either deny or admit the material allegations of the complaint. Such exceptions, along with the

---

53 For the destruction of all but one of the clerks' subpoena books, see Bryson, pp. 111–12. The penalty threatened, but never levied, was £100.

54 Thomas Powell, *The Attourneys Academy* (1623), p. 1.

55 However, up to the reforms of 1706 copy bills were normally sent down to parties answering by commission in the country.

56 George II c. 25. On Chancery's inclusion within the ambit of a process first legislated with respect to the courts of common law, see Stephen C. Yeazell, 'Default and Modern Process', *Legal History in the Making* (1991), eds. W. M. Gordon and T. D. Fergus, esp pp. 129–32.

57 For the relative frequency that defendants were allowed extra time to answer in the later decades of the Court's existence, see below p. 34.

58 As sworn documents, answers from earlier suits might be introduced in evidence in subsequent ones if the party making the answer were no longer alive (just as depositions from witnesses no longer alive or out of the realm might similarly be used). The usual reason for the Court to waive the requirement that the answer be sworn was that the suit was collusive and the plaintiff had petitioned for such a waiver.

59 For the character and frequency of such schedules, see Chapter Four and Table XXII, p. 85.

proposed answer and the bill of complaint, would then be heard and passed upon by the Court.[60] If any of the exceptions were upheld, the defendant was bound to put in a further answer responsive to such exceptions[61]. Once an answer had been submitted, the complainant was required within one term to respond with her/his replication.[62] Failure to meet this deadline entitled the defendant to move to dismiss the bill of complaint. A replication tended to be pro forma, a brief paragraph or two in formulaic terms intended to close out the pleadings (by eschewing any new facts or arguments that the defendant would need to controvert), but the plaintiff in a so-called 'special replication' might introduce new factual allegations, supportive of yet not deviating in essentials from the statements he/she had already made in the bill. To such a replication, the defendant might enter a rejoinder – a reiteration of the principal assertions of his/her answer, with any possible elaborations she/he thought useful in the light of any substantive additions in the plaintiff's replication. Indeed, even further exchanges beyond the replication and rejoinder were allowed under the Exchequer's (and the Chancery's) rules – surrejoinders, rebutters, and surrebutters – but these possibilities were rarely exploited. Indeed, by the eighteenth century, and to a fair measure even earlier, bill, answer, and replication constituted the normal pleadings, followed by the issue by the plaintiff to the defendant of a subpoena to rejoin – a step which would be followed by the beginning of the process of taking depositions.[63]

Not surprisingly, occasions arose when the rules governing the content of replications were felt to be unduly constraining. Thus, the Court would allow the submission of an 'amended' bill (the original bill with interlineations made on it, along with the date of such alterations) – an increasingly common practice in the eighteenth century. The amendment often involved a change in the identity of the parties on the opposing side – the addition of a new defendant as a 'necessary party' (i.e., someone whose interests would be directly affected by a judgement for the plaintiff) or, on occasion, the omission of an individual named in the original bill. Such amendments might also be prompted by material in a defendant's answer. Hence, upon payment of the stipulated fees, an amended bill could also be filed after the defendant's answer. (Indeed, it was possible even after a rule for publication had passed – that is, after the taking of witnesses' depositions – to add new parties if at this stage it became apparent that not all the proper parties were included.) Naturally, such amendment would prolong the pleadings since the defendant, if he/she had already answered, would have to be allowed time to alter his/her answer (under these circumstances, the defendant would also be allowed costs); as a consequence, the date by which the complainant had to file a replication would have to be extended.

60 By contrast, exceptions to answers in Chancery were first referred to a Master to consider. See, for example, the comments of Baron Graham in John v. Dacie (1824), George Price, *Report of Cases . . . in the Court of Exchequer* XIII (1828), 635.

61 Normally, only the subsequent, satisfactory answer would be preserved among the Court's records. Should a defendant fail, after four attempts, to submit a satisfactory answer, the defendant would be liable to proceedings for contempt.

62 As compared to a maximum of three terms in Chancery. To forestall a dismissal, the plaintiff could move for the setting of a date for hearing, could present his replication of the defendant's answer, or could amend his bill (though only once for this purpose). For the possibilities of delay, see Turner v. Calvert (1817), *The English Reports*, vol. 146, 223 (Price, III, 161–3).

63 It should be noted, however, that in the 1819 sample, the only four replications filed in E 112 are all followed by rejoinders from defendants.

However, if the plaintiff had already submitted his replication, new substantive matter coming to his attention could only be incorporated in his case by way of a 'supplemental' bill. Such a supplemental bill could be filed as a matter 'of course' – that is, without the prior permission of the Court.

In the event, all the pleadings, complainant's bill(s), defendant's response(s), and complainant's replication, were supposed to end up on file (usually held together by string put through the top left-hand margin). Not all did so, or if filed remained there, but on the whole the Exchequer apparatus for the keeping of equity pleadings was distinctly superior to that of Chancery, in no small part because of the dispersion of record-keeping responsibilities among the individual Six Clerks in Chancery. Even so, there were significant losses of Exchequer pleadings and other documents, and this phenomenon must be discussed in fuller detail in Chapter Three when we come to consider the individual record classes.[64]

(II) Interlocutory relief and interlocutory process

If a complainant sought an injunction, whether to restrain his opponent from pursuing proceedings in another court (the 'common injunction') or from carrying out some potentially irremediable act before his present suit in Exchequer could be adjudicated (the 'special injunction', e.g., to halt the sale of a book in which the plaintiff held copyright), he/she might do so in his/her bill of complaint or, after filing the bill, by motion to the Court. If the defendant sought permission to answer in the country or failed to appear and to answer promptly, the Court would, at the plaintiff's motion, authorize an injunction as a matter of course.

The force of an Exchequer injunction varied according to where the party enjoined was resident, in the metropolis or in the country. If he/she resided within or close by the metropolis, it would be deemed a breach of the Court's order to proceed 'one step at law' after being served a copy of the writ. Thus, the Exchequer injunction in this form was rather more confining than the normal Chancery injunction which merely inhibited proceedings at law from proceeding to judgement (and execution). The same stricter rule applied to causes where the party was resident in the provinces if filed in Michaelmas or Easter terms (i.e., the terms after the assizes). But if filed in the terms preceding the assizes (Hilary or Trinity), the plaintiff at law was permitted to go to trial at the following assizes and the injunction only stayed judgement and execution.[65] However, once a defendant, wherever resident, had answered, the burden would be on the complainant to show cause for any continuation of the injunction, with such questions being heard by the Court. Should a defendant wish for any reason to seek an injunction (a rather uncommon occurrence), she/he could so move after filing an answer.

While for a variety of reasons, to be discussed in Chapter Two, injunctions increasingly became a staple of Exchequer equity (by contrast to Chancery) and so took up more than one chapter of Fowler's treatise, interlocutory motions – increasingly a feature of Chancery practice and often blamed for spinning out of Chancery causes – seem to have been rather less common in Exchequer equity. While mid-seventeenth century and later critics of Chancery

---

64 See, in general, Bryson, pp. 82–90. Bryson suggests, at p. 86, that 'the records of the equity side of the exchequer have survived virtually intact.'

65 Fowler, I, 259–60; Barton, p. 49.

deplored the multiplication of unnecessary motions as a principal 'cause of long and tedious suits' and Maddock in 1820 detailed 57 distinct types of motions that might be made to the Court, Fowler gives them little heed, devoting but three pages to motions and only a further seven pages to interlocutory and side bar orders (such orders, often involving the scheduling of hearings on pleas, demurrers, and exceptions, were entered without discussion).[66]

(III) Proofs: Interrogatories, Depositions, and Exhibits

The next stage of an equity case, the presentation of proofs, began after the exchange of pleadings had ended, unless the plaintiff was prepared to go to a hearing simply on the strength of the contents of the pleadings (including the attachments submitted by some parties).[67] The principal, though not the invariable, mode of proof was the taking of statements on oath from the witnesses designated by the opposing sides. Such testimony might be reinforced by laying before the Court various kinds of documentary support for the parties' respective claims.

Normally, testimony was taken out of Court (though it was possible with special permission to examine witnesses *viva voce* at the hearing of the cause for a limited number of purposes, as, for example, to authenticate a document). And while the parties themselves were rarely summoned as witnesses (though occasionally some defendants in the case were transmuted into witnesses, by consent), it should be borne in mind that the defendant's answer was on oath and he/she was bound by whatever he/she had therein admitted.[68]

The taking of testimony of witnesses normally residing in or within ten miles of London was the responsibility of one of the individual Examiners serving each of the four Barons.[69] The interrogation of witnesses residing in the provinces was the responsibility of specially-named commissioners from the localities concerned (with each side nominating several individuals, subject to the Court's approval).

Whoever was charged with the taking of testimony, their responsibility was strictly confined to that task. The witnesses were simply asked to answer under oath to lists of written questions (interrogatories) drawn up by the respective parties or their counsel, and much care was usually taken by the opposing sides to formulate their interrogatories in ways that would produce responses supportive of their claims.[70] Each side might also submit interrogatories to be directed to some or all of the witnesses of the opposing side, but they could not cross-examine them in the conventional sense. Rather, the questioner simply put the interrogatories

---

66 Horwitz, *Chancery Equity Records*, p. 15; Fowler, II, 271–6, 392–4. Most proceedings styled motions in Chancery are treated by Fowler under the rubric of 'interlocutory orders'.

67 By opting for this procedure, the plaintiff was in effect conceding the truth of the matters included in the defendant's answer. The Court's consent was required for scheduling a hearing on bill and answer. Note that while it was more common for defendants than plaintiffs to attach accounts or schedules to their pleadings, plaintiffs also did so on occasion. For further discussion of attached schedules, see Chapter Four and Table XXII, p. 85.

68 Fowler, I, 100, stipulates that if a defendant is to be examined as a witness, the plaintiff should not reply to his/her answer.

69 Fowler adds, however, that any of the Barons might personally depose any witness: I, 26.

70 That no little skill was involved in devising the interrogatories is suggested by the publication of the anonymous *Collection of Interrogatories for the Examination of Witnesses in Courts of Equity, as settled by the most eminent Counsel,* penned by 'an old solicitor', and first published in 1775, with a second edition the following year.

to the witnesses, memorialized in writing the answers of the witnesses (the depositions), and then read back their statements to the deponents to assure their accuracy.

Once both sides in a suit had all their witnesses deposed, the Court, at the motion of one of the parties (usually the plaintiff), issued a rule for 'publication', that is, set a day when the depositions in the case were to be 'published' in open court. Only at this stage were the two sides permitted access to the statements of each other's witnesses, although allegations of pre-publication disclosures were occasionally made. At this juncture, either party was free to file exceptions against the credit of the other side's witnesses (provided that the objecting party had not, in effect, 'established' a particular witness by including him or her among its own list of witnesses).

By this stage, too, the parties would have been obliged to bring in any documentary evidence they wished to offer or had sought, usually by motion, from the opposing side. Such materials would be received by the Usher of the Court, as one of his multifarious ministerial tasks. Documentary evidence submitted as exhibits varied in substance depending on the nature of the dispute; it might include title and other property records, account books, or any other materials deemed useful by either side. It might be submitted voluntarily, for instance, via a schedule attached to a defendant's answer, but it might also be produced under a subpoena *duces tecum* upon the motion or petition of the other side. It might also require the testimony of a witness at the hearing to authenticate the document.

The efficacy of the procedures used by the Exchequer and other courts of equity for examining witnesses was frequently criticized in the later seventeenth and eighteenth centuries on a variety of grounds, chiefly the lack of flexibility and also the lack of opportunity to test the witnesses' credibility before the court. And indeed, the court, after reviewing the depositions and any other proofs at a hearing of the cause, might, if in doubt, refer a question of fact to trial at common law on a 'feigned issue', before proceeding to come to a decision informed by a jury's verdict. Just how common this practice was is not easy to determine. Various contemporaries, including a House of Commons committee of 1705–6 and some of the witnesses before the parliamentary inquiry on Chancery in the mid-1820s, stated that such directions were frequently issued by Chancery.[71] Certainly this procedure was understood by both Exchequer and Chancery to be required if the relevant factual question was a rectorial right to tithes or a matter of right in an heir-at-law.

However, the assertion that such 'feigned issues' were common and frequent in the later 1600s and the 1700s applies distinctly more to proceedings in Exchequer than to those in Chancery, as will become evident in our discussion of operating procedure.[72] Here let it be said that such references to jury trials of specific questions, while quite common in tithe suits, were by no means confined to them. The procedure in Exchequer was for a party to 'settle' an issue via the 'Office of Pleas', which would then arrange for trial either at the assizes, or at the London and Middlesex sittings, or occasionally at the bar of the Exchequer.[73]

---

71 These are the sources relied upon by Sir William Holdsworth, *A History of English Law,* IX (1926), 357 and note 3. See also *Lord Nottingham's 'Manual'*, p. 220.

72 See below, p. 32. And for problems in transporting equity standards of evidence into jury trials at common law see below fn. 90.

73 By contrast, the trying of a feigned issue out of Chancery required the parties to have recourse to the officers of one of the central common law courts.

(IV) Hearing, Deputy's Report, and Decree

With depositions taken and 'published', the stage was now set for the fixing of a date for the hearing before the Barons. But in practice, the road was not so smooth. For one thing, if any party had died in the months (or years) of the intervening stages of the case, the suit would have 'abated' and would have had to be restarted by way of filing a bill of revivor to reinstate the cause in the posture it had stood at the time of the death. The same requirement applied if a plaintiff who was a single woman married, for in that case her husband (by analogy to the common law doctrine of *coverture*) was treated as a necessary party. Conversely, a married woman who was widowed had the option of putting in a new bill or answer. Often, a bill of revivor would be accompanied by a supplemental bill to enable the plaintiff to add to or to enlarge her/his pleadings.

As death or, in the case of a woman, marriage (or remarriage), not infrequently interrupted equity suits before the Barons, so progress to the hearing of a cause was often slowed by the Court's burden of business. The Court could only hear so many causes in a day (a dozen was the norm in the eighteenth century), and even with a day fixed on the Court's lists there might be further delays when parties (or sometimes their counsel) failed to attend.

Beyond the problems of scheduling the hearing and securing the requisite attendance, it was not uncommon for hearings to end without a definitive resolution, at least in detail. Frequently, after reviewing the pleadings, the depositions, and any other evidence submitted, the presiding judges would pronounce on the general issue and then make a 'reference': that is, refer the cause to the Deputy Remembrancer with instruction to review some or all of the facts of the matter in the light of the judgement on the general issue and then to report back to the Court on how the judgement should be implemented, e.g., how a disputed estate should be handled in terms of ascertaining of debts, marshalling of assets, reconciling conflicting claims among the beneficiaries, and providing for the guardianship and upbringing of minor beneficiaries.

It was, then, the responsibility of the parties or their legal advisers to attend the Deputy Remembrancer.[74] In principle, his task was to inquire into disputed or simply relevant factual questions, not to get involved with the rights and wrongs of the matter, but this was not always a line easy to observe. In any case, it was open to the Deputy not only to review the proofs in detail but also, if he saw fit, to question on oath, via written interrogatories, any of the witnesses or the parties.[75] Drafts of the report, when prepared, were then to be submitted for comments to each side.[76]

As the opposing parties might try to influence the Deputy's view of the matter by their own or their legal representatives' presentations, so it was open to them, if they objected to the substance of the report as prepared, to lay exceptions (confined to submissions previously

74 Parties' repeated failures to attend scheduled proceedings before the Deputy led the Court in 1764 to authorize the Deputy to proceed *ex parte* under such circumstances; Fowler I, 278.

75 The parties, in turn, might submit interrogatories for the questioning of witnesses; Fowler, II, 294–5, 285–93. The Deputy was also empowered to have recourse to newspaper advertisements for creditors' claims, for legacies, etc.

76 The practice manuals distinguish between general and separate reports, the latter thought by some of the bench to be a cause of unduly protracting cases: Fowler, II, 330 ff; Baron Graham in Hare v. Ruscombe (1824), *The English Reports,* vol. 148, 43 (M'Cleland, p. 102).

made to the Deputy) before the Court and have them argued there. The Court might confirm the report or send it back to the Deputy to reconsider in light of some or all of the objections.

Thus, for those causes which involved review of a complex pattern of facts or necessitated detailed plans of implementation, the Deputy's proceedings could be as important in practice as the Court's decisions were in principle. Once the Deputy's report was approved by the Court, a supplementary decretal order incorporating its results would usually be entered.[77]

At this juncture, it was open to either party to have the decretal order, as registered in the Court's records, specially enrolled on parchment. Enrolment was a discretionary step and required the payment of extra fees. It had the advantage of limiting challenges to the Court's decision. Until a decree was enrolled, it technically had the force only of an interlocutory order; it could be altered upon a rehearing or sometimes even on motion. Rehearings, indeed, appear to have become increasingly frequent, and there were repeated complaints during the eighteenth century of the delays they caused. But once a decree was enrolled, it gained a greater degree of finality. Challenges to it in the Exchequer could ordinarily only be made by way of a bill of review. Those seeking reconsideration via a bill of review were limited to evidence before the Court at the time of the original decree (unless they could show cause why any new evidence could not have been available to them on the earlier occasion) and also had to show that they had conformed to the terms of the original decree.[78] In these ways, enrolment could create a substantial barrier to any attempt by the losing side to reopen the cause and so might be worth the additional costs and efforts to the winning party.[79]

Finally, it was open to parties who failed to get satisfaction from the Barons of the Exchequer to contemplate an appeal to the House of Lords. Such appeals were expensive and not lightly undertaken, but from the early seventeenth century the Lords were prepared to review proceedings in the English central courts (and subsequently in those of Scotland and Ireland, too).[80] The grounds for appeal to the Lords were the same as for the proceeding by bill of review – that is, the challenging party had to show that the decree itself contained disabling error. Moreover, the appellant was not allowed to allege any new matter (save in exceptional circumstances) and must have shown good faith by conforming to the terms of the decree he/she was now challenging. Yet however difficult and expensive an appeal to the Lords would be, since the cause would be reviewed by all the peers and since the common law judges might exert a considerable influence, counsel might judge it preferable to a bill of review.

(V) Post-decree proceedings

Post-decree proceedings, apart from rehearings and bills of review (and appeals to the House of Lords), mainly involved the taxation of costs to the losing side by the Deputy (if requested),

---

77 Note Fowler's support of the view that it was only necessary for the party to have the second or final decree (incorporating the Deputy's report) enrolled: II, 237–8.

78 The Court was prepared to make limited exceptions to these requirements when what was sought was an alteration of the enrolled decree in order to correct mistakes of copying and computation; [Richard Boote], *The Solicitor's Practice in the High Court of Chancery Epitomized* (5th edn. 1782), p. 19.

79 For the frequency of enrolments, see below, Table II, p. 33.

80 For the invention of the appeal to the Lords, see James S. Hart, *Justice upon Petition: The House of Lords and the Reformation of Justice 1621–1675* (1991).

processes of enforcement against a recalcitrant loser, and/or requests for adjustments to the terms of decrees necessitated usually by changes of circumstance or by omissions or mistakes in the decree itself. Parties were most likely to come back to Court for 'further directions' on a decree in situations where the decree itself called for continuing action over months and years – most notably, in cases involving the administration of estates.

D. Observations upon Procedure in Practice

(I) Some recurring features

While descriptions of equity practice in Exchequer, as found in manuals for practitioners and other contemporary works (including works on Chancery), provide considerable insight into process and the kind of documents that a suit might generate, a survey of the course of suits – based on samples and selections drawn from the records – serves both to amplify and to qualify these general accounts. Most instructive are the results of 'tracing' cases from beginning to end – a process carried out for two of our four chronological samples (1685 and 1819 – 150 cases each) and 258 causes heard by Chief Baron Ward in the 1690s. All told, these 558 cases, over three-quarters of them from the first century of the Court's general equitable jurisdiction, provide a good deal of detailed information on aspects of court process that the earlier manuals fail to supply.

A brief example will illustrate the usefulness of these data. It concerns the relationship in practice between the dual requirement that a defendant 'appear' (formally acknowledge the jurisdiction of the Court) and 'answer' (respond by plea, demurrer, disclaimer or answer) to the complainant's bill. Records of appearance do not survive for the seventeenth century, but they are extant for the suits in the 1819 sample. All told, 113 defendants are recorded in E 107/16 as appearing in the 150 suits of the 1819 sample. But of these 113, 25 did not submit any answer. Moreover, 15 other defendants answered without ever appearing – or at least being recorded as appearing. Two questions thus arise: (a) do these data reflect clerical (or other) omissions from the appearance records? and (b) if these discrepancies are not a function of defects of the record-keeping process, was the Court cognizant that defendants were answering without first appearing? No answer is possible, but at the least we are cautioned against relying on the appearance books as a complete listing of defendants.[81]

In broader terms, using the data derived from the 558 traced suits, it is possible to document the course of suits with some degree of specificity. The first point to remark, as noted above, is how high a proportion of suits never went beyond the pleadings, or even beyond the bill of complaint, and how few reached the decree stage (see Table I, p. 31).[82]

---

81 Compare Milhous and Hume, 'Eighteenth-century Equity Lawsuits', p. 237.
82 For purposes of our analysis, a suit dismissed without hearing (because of the plaintiff's failure to proceed in his/her suit) is treated as not going beyond the pleadings.

Table I: Suits that never went beyond the bill of complaint and those that never went beyond the pleadings [83]

	Total Suits	**Bill only**	**Bill and Pleadings only**	**Bill, Pleadings and Decree**
1685	150	53	118	15
1819	150	45	124	23

In the face of these data, we can only presume that the act of initiating legal proceedings by filing a bill (coupled, usually, with the service of the subpoena to appear and to answer) sufficed to bring the two parties together and led to some sort of informal settlement of the quarrel. Out-of-court settlements are, indeed, a familiar feature of the litigation process both in the twentieth and in earlier centuries. But just how often the abandonment by the plaintiff of his/her suit before the defendant even answered was the result of an agreement is impossible to calculate; usually, out-of-court settlements were not reported to the Court and hence do not appear in its records.

What is apparent is that equity proceedings in Exchequer, like those in Chancery but with even greater frequency, were likely to terminate well short of a hearing, much less a decree. Of the 300 suits in the 1685 and 1819 Exchequer samples, 242 or 80.7% never went beyond the pleadings, as compared to 73.2% of the 1685 and 1819 Chancery samples (altogether, 216 of 295).[84] To put it slightly differently, only a small minority of equity suits ever got to the stage of a hearing on the main question in dispute and hence to the issuance of a decree.

Given the infrequency which suits in the 1685 and 1819 Exchequer samples survived beyond the pleadings stage, it is useful to have at our disposal another body of data with which to analyse the Court's procedures in subsequent stages of litigation. These cases are drawn from the 258 suits (including 81 tithe cases and 19 suits brought by the Attorney-General) set down for hearing before the Court between Michaelmas 1695 and Trinity 1697 and recorded for that purpose in the 'cause papers' surviving among Chief Baron Edward Ward's manuscripts at Lincoln's Inn.[85]

We may begin this discussion of procedures in the proof stage by noting that it was possible to proceed directly from the pleadings to a hearing, at the plaintiff's discretion. However, in opting for this course the plaintiff was held to be admitting the truth of the defendant's answer, and most plaintiffs thought it the better part of wisdom to assemble proofs to present to the Barons to support their claims.

As we have earlier observed, the principal form of proof before the Exchequer, as in Chancery, was the written testimony of witnesses. Only 158 of the Ward cases culminated in decrees; of these, three-quarters (102 of 132, or 77.2%) were preceded by the taking of depositions, a rather higher proportion than in our sample Chancery suits of 1685 and 1785 (29 of 60 or 48.3%).[86] And just as recourse to witnesses' depositions appears to have been rather

---

83 Bill and pleadings only include bills only. Note, too, that in each sample a number of suits proceeded to the proofs stage without ever culminating in a decree (17 in 1685, 3 in 1819).

84 See Table VI below, p. 36.

85 Lincoln's Inn Library Misc. Ms. 511 and ff. (especially 512, 514–16, and 559). It should be noted that 'cause papers' for most of the rest of Ward's tenure on the Exchequer Bench also survive in this collection.

86 Occasionally, of course, depositions were taken in suits that failed to result in a decree.

more common in Exchequer, so, too, was the sending of issues of fact to be tried before juries at common law. In neither central court of equity was this a common procedure, but it was certainly more frequent in Exchequer than in Chancery.[87] All told in the 158 Ward causes, seventeen (10.8%) were sent for jury trial on specified issues, either at the bar of the Court of Exchequer, at the sittings for London or Middlesex, or at the county assizes.[88] The questions involved were diverse: only three fell within the rubric of a matter of right in an heir at law or in a rector; the other fourteen included such diverse issues as relief from conditional bonds, the maintenance of corporate privileges, and the specific performance of agreements to convey.

Without unduly stressing the differences between the two central courts of equity, it may be worth considering why Exchequer (even without reckoning in tithe suits) made so much more frequent use of the referral of specific questions to jury trials than did Chancery. The first point to note is that Exchequer was not using the jury as a substitute for the deposition process; rather, in most instances (15 of the 27) recourse to jury trial came only *after* depositions had been gathered; moreover, it was common for the Court to stipulate that depositions already taken might be used at trial at common law. The second point to observe is that the Barons did not feel bound by the resultant jury verdicts.[89] It was always open to the loser at law to argue, and some did successfully, that the verdict was problematic, whether as a result of juror misconduct or of the availability of new evidence or simply of the jury's mis-evaluation of the evidence before it, and hence that the issue should either be submitted to another jury or settled in some other fashion (e.g., arbitration). Furthermore, in coming to the decision as to whether the initial verdict had been a 'good' one, the Barons were apt to depend on the opinion of the presiding judge at trial.[90] In fact, of the 17 Ward causes which went to trial at law, four were sent back a second time, and one eventually went to three juries.[91] Finally, we may note that litigants in Exchequer could relatively painlessly arrange trials at common law, thanks to the presence in the Exchequer of the 'Office of Pleas'; no such facility existed in Chancery, and a litigant seeking to organize a trial at law would have to have recourse to the officers of one of the central common law courts.

87 Of the 246 Chancery sample suits in toto from 1685 and 1785 there were only five references to the common law; Horwitz, *Chancery Equity Records*, p. 21

88 Of the 81 Ward tithe cases in the original total of 258 but excluded from the 158 under examination here, 16 engendered references to common law trials.

89 And this despite the fact that it would appear to have been the norm for 'feigned issues' at law from the Exchequer to be heard by 'special' juries – i.e., juries empanelled by special procedures aimed at returning bodies of men of rather higher socio-economic standing than ordinary jurors.

90 See in Priaulx v. Stone, Baron Powis acquainting the court that the trial judge Eyre had 'declared the verdict not to his satisfaction but that the cause was proper for a new trial': E 126/16, 26 Nov. 1696. See also the case of Carter v. Salt of Hilary 1714/15: upon the report of the verdict at law, the losing side made a motion for a new trial, but it was dismissed after opposing counsel cited Chief Justice King's 'opinion of the verdict and his notes taken upon the trial to the following effect' (Harvard Law School MS. 1216, read on fiche compiled by J.H. Baker [2R 2]). Differences between ordinary common law trials and those on feigned issues directed by the courts of equity are analysed at length in the House of Lords' deliberations in Bullen v. Michel in 1816; note especially the comments of Lord Chancellor Eldon and Lord Redesdale (the former John Mitford) in *The English Reports*, vol. 146, 399 ff. (Price, II, 466–9, 482–3, 490–4).

91 Horwitz, 'Chancery's "Younger Sister"', pp. 177–8.

It would appear, then, that both recourse to witnesses and reference to common law trials were more common in Exchequer than in Chancery (even leaving aside the frequency of references to juries in tithe cases). But, of course, given the relatively small minority of cases that proceeded beyond the pleadings stage, even in Exchequer the taking of depositions figures in only a small percentage of all suits filed while recourse to common law trials proves even more unusual. Similarly, no more than one suit in ten or fewer required delegation to the Deputy Remembrancer, whether that was to compute tithes owing, report on the assets of a deceased, or tax costs to the losing party: in 1685, the services of the Deputy in this capacity were utilized in 10 suits, in 1819 in 15.

(II) Change over time

Clearly, there were a good many constants in Exchequer equity process and practice as between the later seventeenth and early nineteenth centuries. But there were also some significant changes. Some changes made for greater simplification.

One concerns the parties' use of the process of enrolment of equity decrees on the King's Remembrancer's memoranda rolls (E 159). As a comparison of E 126 (decrees entered) with E 159 (decrees enrolled) reveals (see Table II), enrolment was not uncommon in the later seventeenth century but increasingly infrequent thereafter as few winning parties appear to have been prepared to pay the additional fees involved.

To explain these data is not easy, but analogy with Chancery helps since a more or less similar situation pertained – that is, enrolment was common but still the exception in Chancery in the seventeenth century, and quite exceptional by the early nineteenth century.[92] Two possibilities with respect to the downturn of enrolments in Chancery may well also apply to Exchequer. One is the Court's own discouragement of enrolment on the grounds that there was a high risk of technical error in the enrolment process which would only create complications in the event of a bill of review or an appeal to the Lords.[93] The second is the new availability from the seventeenth century onwards of the appeal to the House of Lords.[94]

Just as the enrolled decree became a vanishing species, so did the so-called 'copy bill' – the copy of the bill of complaint that accompanied the commission issued to take a defendant's answer in the country. Thanks to the statute of 1706 (4–5 Anne c. 3), the

Table II: Enrolments of Exchequer equity decrees

Decrees entered (E 126)		Decrees enrolled (E 159)	
1685	69	1685	21
1735	70	1735–44	35
1785	126	1785–94	2
1819	117	1819–25	11

92 Horwitz, *Chancery Equity Records*, pp. 27–8.

93 Samuel Turner, *An Epitome of the Practice of the High Court of Chancery* (1809), p. 37.

94 Note, however, that appeals of Exchequer equity decisions to the House of Lords rarely numbered more than one or two a year through the eighteenth century.

requirement on the defendant to pay for the copy bill was abolished on the grounds that it was an unnecessary charge and of value only to the clerks who had to be paid for copying it out.

In other respects, however, more paper and parchment were being generated with the passage of time. The bills of complaint of the 1685 Exchequer sample are virtually all original bills: there is only one amended bill among them and no supplemental bills. By comparison, the bills in the 1819 sample include thirteen amended bills and five supplemental bills. And just as plaintiffs in the later sample were more likely to be altering their bills to take account of changing circumstances (or aspects of defendants' answers), so defendants in 1819 were also more likely to back up their answers with a species of proof. This was the schedule, attached to the answer (or sometimes to the bill), and giving a detailed account (often in pounds, shillings, and pence) of the parties' claims. Thirty answers (and three bills of complaint) from the 1819 sample append such schedules by comparison to only thirteen from the 1685 group.

Finally, in isolating changes over time in the conduct of equity litigation, we may observe that contemporary laments about the growing slowness of the equity courts were not without foundation. The reasons for this development, and an in-depth comparison with Chancery, will be discussed in Chapter Two, once we have explored the Exchequer's subject-matter jurisdiction in equity and changes in that jurisdiction over time. For the moment, we can illustrate this slowing of Exchequer equity process in very simple fashion by measuring the length of the interval between the filing of a complainant's bill and of the defendant's answer.[95] In the 1685 Exchequer sample, the great majority of defendants submitted their answers either in the same term that the bill of complaint was filed or in the next succeeding term (78.6%). By contrast, in the 1819 sample, less than half (48.8%) of the defendants filed their answers in either the same or the succeeding term, and over 15% managed to evade putting-in answers until four or more terms after the filing of the bill. Given the Court's unwillingness to enforce its rules about the speed with which answers were to be filed, not to mention other forms of laxness, it is hardly surprising that the proportion of Exchequer equity suits lasting over two years rose more than threefold from 8% in the 1685 sample to 26.7% in the 1819 sample.

In a variety of dimensions, then, the Court of Exchequer's operation by the later eighteenth and early nineteenth centuries differed significantly from the patterns two centuries earlier. And as will become clear in Chapter Two, so did the subject matter of Exchequer suits and the identity of Exchequer litigants.

---

95 Our computations exclude those suits in which there were either no answers made or answers made at different times by multiple defendants.

CHAPTER TWO
The Equity Jurisdiction of the Court of Exchequer, 1649–1841

This chapter considers the volume, scope, and character of the Court of Exchequer's business over its two centuries of operation as a general equitable jurisdiction. The aim is to furnish guideposts and gauges to the range and type of disputes found in the Court's records, at various points distributed across these two centuries, as indicators to what it may be profitable for the searcher to pursue. The chapter also includes an analysis of the social and geographical origins of the plaintiffs and defendants: what sorts of people brought bills of complaint into the Court, who were these suits directed against, and how the character of the litigants changed over time in terms of status/occupation or geographical origin. Finally, this chapter offers a tentative and partial answer as to why certain types of plaintiffs, seeking certain remedies, preferred to lay their complaints in Exchequer rather than in Chancery.

A. The Volume of the Exchequer's Equitable Business

Thanks to the survival of the bill books kept by the clerical staff of the Court, it is easy enough to tabulate the number of suits initiated in any given time period. The bill books are organized by reign, and Bryson's study provides totals and annual averages by reign. All told, he counted some 90,072 bills between 1649 and 1841 yielding a yearly average of 467 new bills filed. At the same time, his count also reveals substantial fluctuations by reign, with average yearly totals rising from a level of 331 during James I's reign, to 464 during the Interregnum, 571 over Charles II's reign, 650 in James II's reign, and 740 during William III's reign. Thereafter, a decline in business set in, at first gradual and then more rapid: 715 new bills per annum during Anne's reign, 687 yearly during George I's reign, slumping to 352 over George II's reign. Over George III's reign, spanning six decades, a partial recovery is signalled by an annual average of 427. But this recovery proved evanescent, as in the last 20 years of the Court's life the annual average fell to 329 – that is, virtually the same level as had prevailed in the early seventeenth century before the expansion of the Court's jurisdiction.

In broad terms, the pattern of ebbs and flows of Exchequer equity business from the Restoration to the early nineteenth century tend to resemble trends in Chancery business during this era. In particular, both central courts of equity suffered a serious decline of business from late-seventeenth/early-eighteenth century peaks to mid-eighteenth century depths. And both courts experienced a partial recovery over the course of George III's long reign. Moreover, a similar pattern is discernible in the volume of civil business in the central courts of common law over roughly the same period.[1] But if both central courts of equity were afflicted by the same secular trends between the later seventeenth and early nineteenth centuries, their experience was not altogether identical.

---

1 And to add to the signs of decline, there was also a sharp fall in felony indictments in the period.

Table III: Chancery and Exchequer new bills for four sample years

	1685	**1735**	**1785**	**1819**
Chancery	5660	3240	1544	2335
Exchequer	650	265	450	374

As Table III illustrates, the ratio between Chancery and Exchequer new equity bills per annum was roughly eight and one-half to one in the mid-1680s, twelve to one in the mid-1730s, three and one-half to one in 1785, and six to one in 1819. That is to say, Exchequer suffered an earlier and sharper decline than Chancery, but also recovered more quickly and somewhat more successfully. Thus, comparing the data for 1819 to those for 1685, it is apparent that while both courts had significantly lower volumes of new business per annum at the later date, Exchequer had more than held its own in relative terms *vis-à-vis* Chancery.

New bills per annum are, to be sure, only one measure of the case load of Exchequer (and of Chancery), particularly as many complainants, as we have earlier observed, appear to have taken no further action or to have halted proceedings before any decision on the matter in dispute was reached by the court. As Table IV indicates, a high proportion of bills included in our chronological samples never even elicited answers from the defendants – that is, there is no record of proceedings in such suits beyond the complainants' initial filing.

Table IV: Proportions of bills-only suits from the four sample Exchequer sets (each 150)

1685	**1735**	**1785**	**1819**
53 35%	69 46%	82 55%	45 30%

By comparison, the proportions of bills-only suits in Chancery, while still substantial, were significantly lower throughout the period.

Table V: Proportions of bills-only suits in the four sample Chancery sets

1685	**1735**	**1785**	**1819**
33 of 146 22.6%	73 of 294 24.8%	35 of 140 25.0%	33 of 149 22.1%

Concomitantly, though in both courts only a minority of suits culminated in a judicial decision on the substance, in Exchequer that minority was significantly smaller than in Chancery.

Table VI: Suits culminating in decrees in the traced pleadings for Exchequer and Chancery

	1685	**1785**	**1819**
Exchequer	15 of 150 10.0%	(Not traced)	23 of 150 15.3%
Chancery	26 of 146 17.8%	36 of 140 25.7%	53 of 149 35.6%

These data suggest that despite the two courts' employment of largely-similar procedures and despite their concurrent jurisdictions there may well have been significant differences in the origins and types of business they entertained and/or in the types of litigants who invoked their jurisdiction.

B. The Geographical Origin of Suits and Litigants

The Exchequer attracted equity suits from all the counties of England and Wales, and the clerks of the Exchequer Office filed the incoming bills mainly by county while grouping bills from the City of London and those from the county of Middlesex together.[2] Their rule of thumb appears to have been to assign county designation either by the location of any tangible property in dispute or, if that was not self-evident from a quick perusal of the bill, by the place of residence of the first-named plaintiff.[3] Because it was possible, then, for a bill with a London or Middlesex plaintiff to be filed under some other county – e.g., a tithe dispute in Herefordshire with a London plaintiff might well be filed under Herefordshire – the match between first plaintiff's place of residence and the county of filing is not complete.[4]

Bearing in mind this feature of Exchequer record-keeping, it is nonetheless possible to discern some striking shifts over time in the geographical composition of the Court's equity business. In the first place, there is the growing proportion of bills emanating from the London metropolitan area[5] as compared to the rest of England and Wales.

Table VII: Proportions of Exchequer equity suits from London and Middlesex v. the rest of England and Wales[6]

	1685	1735	1785	1819
	%	%	%	%
London and Middlesex	20.2	29.9	33.8	35.3
Other	79.8	70.1	66.2	64.7

2 Other noteworthy particularities were to file Cambridgeshire and Huntingdonshire together (originally a joint county with a single sheriff), and to list a number of more important provincial towns with their respective counties as Chester with Cheshire and Exeter with Devonshire (as illustrated in the list from E 192/133 extracted in fn. 3 below).

3 Bryson, pp. 106–7; Fowler, I, 130; Samuel Turner, *An Epitome of the practice of the Equity Side of Exchequer* (2nd edn., 1806), p. 18. Though Bryson suggests to the contrary, it would appear that each of the six sworn clerks (i.e., not the Secondaries), had his own group of counties for purposes of filing: see E 192/133, unfoliated: 'The Account of each Gentleman's Division" [mid-eighteenth century] – 'Fowler [Mr. Price's, crossed out]: Berwick, Chester, Cheshire, Dover [a Cinque Port listed under 'C'], Bedfordshire, Buckinghamshire, Bristol [for administrative purposes, a county of itself], Cambridgeshire, Huntingdonshire, Cornwall, Cumberland, Exeter, Devonshire'.

4 In our four chronological samples of 150 each, we find Londoners as first-named plaintiffs in a total of 18 provincial cases; conversely, we find provincial residents or residents of rural Middlesex as first-named plaintiffs in 30 'London and Middlesex' bills (most frequently in the last of the four samples). Reliance on the clerks' categorizations tend to enlarge marginally the proportion of metropolitan cases in the 1785 and 1819 samples with the opposite effect in the 1685 and 1735 samples. See also Table XIX, p. 50.

5 By the London metropolis is meant the medieval City along with the built-up parts of Middlesex (whose size considerably expanded between the later 17th and early 19th centuries) and also metropolitan Surrey (essentially Southwark).

6 Derived from our own counts of bill book entries, which vary somewhat from those in Table III, p. 36.

Secondly, if we group individual counties into regions as defined by the assize circuits, it emerges that while the provinces as a whole (including the Welsh counties) lost ground in relative terms to the metropolis over this period, not all parts of the country suffered equally. Between the 1680s and the 1810s, the fall-off in percentage of bills filed was sharpest for the Home Counties (Bedfordshire, Berkshire, Buckinghamshire, Essex, Hertfordshire), followed by East Anglia (Cambridgeshire, Huntingdonshire, Norfolk, and Suffolk), and the southwest (Cornwall, Devon, Dorset, Gloucestershire, Somerset, and Wiltshire). On the other hand, the north (Cumberland, Durham, Lancashire, Westmorland, Northumberland, and Yorkshire) gained noticeably, with business from this circuit rising by nearly 50%.[7]

Some similar trends are evident in the geographical mix of Chancery's case load. For one, between 1685 and 1819, the proportion of London and Middlesex suits rose from 25.3% to 37.6%.[8] For another, East Anglia was the region suffering the heaviest proportional decline over the same period. In Chancery, however, by contrast to the Exchequer, the northern region also incurred a major decline over the same period.[9]

To account for these shifts in the geographical origins of equity suits heard in the central courts is at best speculative, particularly bearing in mind that both courts suffered from a sharp downturn in business extending over most of the eighteenth century, and that their subsequent recovery left them attracting significantly lower totals of new bills of complaint in the late 1810s by comparison to the mid-1680s. Thus, the proportional growth of suits emanating from London and Middlesex will be of greater moment if we can establish that this trend meant a different mix of types of suits, of types of remedies sought, and/or of types of litigants.

C. Subject-Matter Jurisdiction

(I) Tithe disputes

Although Chancery's and Exchequer's equity jurisdictions were concurrent (any suit that could be filed in one could be filed in the other), the profile of Exchequer's business, as gauged by sampling bills of complaint and grouping them by subject matter, was marked by some distinctive features. Above all, there is the considerable, though declining, number of tithe disputes litigated in Exchequer.[10]

---

7 We have adopted this procedure to facilitate comparisons with C. W. Brooks, *Lawyers, Litigation and English Society since 1450* (1998), pp. 37–8.

8 Chancery bills of complaint were not kept on a county-by-county basis; these geographical data have been tabulated by first plaintiff's place of residence.

9 For the decline in suits from East Anglia at common law, see Brooks, *Lawyers,* p. 38.

10 Other approaches to gauging subject matter would be to focus on decrees or reported cases. Tithe suits are over-represented, by comparison to the bill samples, in those sources (especially in Exchequer printed cases of the periods overlapping the samples), thus contributing to the traditional perception of Exchequer as the principal venue for such suits. Tithe cases amounted to 21.3% of the four sample sets of bills (128 of 600), 43.8% (149 of 340) of printed cases, 34.1% (139 of 408) of manuscript cases, and 29.2% (91 of 312) of decrees. For these data sets, see Appendix Two. For the under-representation of business cases, see fn. 19 below.

Table VIII: Tithe suits in Exchequer samples (each sample = 150)

1685	1735	1785	1819
54 36%	33 22%	23 15%	18 12%

By comparison, tithe disputes, though not unknown in Chancery, were few and far between. Thus, in the 1685 and 1735 Chancery samples combined, only four of 544 suits involved tithes (as compared to 87 of 300 in the 1685 and 1735 Exchequer samples). Exchequer's extensive jurisdiction in tithe cases predated the Court's mid-seventeenth century expansion. Before the breach with Rome, such disputes had been mainly handled by the church courts, and throughout our period they still retained a jurisdiction. But after the Henrician dissolution of the religious orders (which led to many appropriated tithes being transferred to laymen) and after the incorporation of the Court of Augmentations (the body originally created to control the Crown's acquisitions from the Church) into the reorganized Exchequer during the 1550s, the Barons of the Exchequer took on an increasingly important role.[11]

Tithe cases were not strictly equitable causes, but they were handled via English bill process. And, as Fowler remarked in retrospect, 'without assuming an exclusive jurisdiction', the Court gradually acquired 'a peculiar jurisdiction, by its numerous decisions upon this species of property' so that its decrees 'are now resorted to as of the highest legal authority'.[12]

While Exchequer's case load throughout included a much higher proportion of tithe suits than did Chancery's, it is instructive that the decline over time in tithe suits in Exchequer parallels the growth of the proportion of its business emanating from London and Middlesex. The two developments are partially inter-related, as throughout the period tithe cases originating in London were, for the most part, not litigated in Exchequer (or in Chancery) but in the Lord Mayor's Court, as provided for by the statute of 37 Henry VIII c. 12.[13] Thus, an analysis of all London and Middlesex suits in Exchequer for 1685 and 1785 (some 345 in total, of which 85 are also included in the samples for these years) reveals that of this total, only six involve tithes, and all these six emanated from Middlesex, not from the City.[14]

---

11 In Lord Chancellor Nottingham's view, the Exchequer's heavy involvement in tithe dispute derived from the Court of Augmentations; Fowler, I, 5.

12 Fowler, I, 3–4. Note, too, the observation of [William Booth], *The Compleat Solicitor Performing His Duty* (1666), p. 388, that it was common for clerics to exhibit English bills for small tithes 'to make the defendants set them forth upon oath'.

13 Nonetheless, as Professor Bryson has pointed out to me, there are a few London tithe decrees printed in the four volumes of Hutton Wood, mostly for the early period: Hutton Wood, *A Collection of Decrees by the Court of Exchequer in Tithe Causes, from the Usurpation to the Present Time* (4 vols., 1798–9). This reflects Exchequer's retention of a concurrent jurisdiction over London tithe cases; Charles Ellis, *A Treatise on the Pleadings in Suits for Tithes in Equity* (1821), p. 81. And see Thomas G. Western, *Cases relating to the Tithes of the City of London* (1823).

14 The pleadings in these 345 suits will be calendared in volume 35 (2000) of the London and Middlesex Record Society.

(II) Injunctive proceedings

As tithe disputes are a marked, if declining, feature of Exchequer's provincial business, so the prevalence of 'common injunction' suits before the Barons also helps to differentiate the case load of the two central courts of equity. 'Common injunction' proceedings, as noted in Chapter One, were bills filed by plaintiffs who were either already being sued at common law (often over credit or business transactions) or who were acting in anticipation of such suits; such plaintiffs sought the Court's orders to enjoin actions against them at common law until their opponents appeared before the Barons and answered their bills of complaint. Such proceedings were not unknown in Chancery, but they were relatively more frequent in Exchequer, as indicated in Table IX.

Table IX: 'Common Injunction' suits in Exchequer and Chancery samples (without tithe cases)

	1685	**1785**
EXCHEQUER	22 of 96: 22.9%	61 of 127: 48.0%
(A) London and Middlesex	12 of 33: 36.4%	37 of 51: 72.6%
(B) Provincial	10 of 63: 15.9%	24 of 76: 31.6%
CHANCERY[15]	25 of 250: 10.0%	12 of 140: 8.6%

On the one hand, Table IX unquestionably bears out the testimony in 1840 before the House of Lords of the barrister James Wigram. He informed the peers:[16]

> When I used to draw more bills in the Court of Exchequer, a large proportion . . . were bills for the mere purpose of obtaining injunctions to restrain proceedings at [common] law. If a party wished to use a Court of Equity as the means of defeating a plaintiff at Law, he generally had recourse to the Court of Exchequer.

Exchequer's advantage, by comparison with Chancery, was that its injunctions were broader in scope and also might delay proceedings in other courts for a longer span of time. A Chancery injunction would not inhibit another court's coming to judgement but simply suspend the execution of that judgement; an Exchequer injunction 'stops all further proceedings, in whatever state the cause may be.' Moreover, since the Barons of the Exchequer went on circuit twice yearly whereas the Chancery remained open for much of that time, it was generally quicker and easier for defendants in injunction matters to get a hearing on a Chancery injunction than on one issued by the Exchequer.[17]

On the other hand, it is also apparent from Table IX that requests for common injunctions in Exchequer were much more frequent in London and Middlesex causes than in provincial ones. This finding, in turn, suggests two further related points: first, that London

---

15 The comparable figures for Chancery for 1735 are 40 of 294 (13.6%). For more data on common injunctions in Exchequer, see Tables XII, XIV, and XVI on pp. 43, 45 and 46.

16 As quoted in Horwitz, 'Chancery's "Younger Sister"', p. 175 and n.51. See also the comment of counsel in Rolfe v. Burke (1827), Edward Yonge and John Jervis, *Report of Cases . . . in the Courts of Exchequer and Exchequer Chamber*, I (1828), 405: 'the Exchequer injunction is universally understood in the profession, to be more beneficially comprehensive than Chancery's.' For one solicitor's description of such proceedings, see E 140/145 – letter books of James Elderton, solicitor of Clifford's Inn, book 3, p.10, letter of 9 May 1793.

17 Barton, *Historical Treatise*, p. 52.

and Middlesex suits may have more frequently involved credit and related transactions; secondly, that London and Middlesex suitors may have more commonly been engaged in business and trade.[18] Let us keep these possibilities in mind as we turn to explore the kinds of disputes (apart from tithes) litigated in Exchequer as English bills.

(III) Subject matter of suits apart from tithes

Five main subject-groupings have been employed in categorizing the sample Exchequer equity suits:

(1) estate [testamentary and intestacy] matters;
(2) landholding and land transactions;
(3) *inter-vivos* trusts;
(4) debts and bonds; and
(5) business transactions.

These are 'artificial' in the sense that courts of equity were not constrained by the common law 'forms of action' and had no need to classify their business. And their artificiality may be exaggerated by employing them to make comparisons across two centuries.

In broad terms, suits classed as estate matters concern issues generated by wills and intestacies – above all, claims for payment of legacies and for performance of other provisions of wills (including testamentary trusts). Other significant sub-categories under the estate rubric include suits brought to secure the assets of a deceased, suits disputing the validity of testaments, and suits concerning charitable bequests (with the Attorney-General often a plaintiff in such cases, usually acting 'at the relation' (i.e., *ex rel.*) of the designated beneficiaries.

Suits categorized as related to landholding and other real property questions include, most prominently, demands for specific performance of agreements to convey, mortgage foreclosures and redemptions, and claims to land with requests for remedies for defective transfers (i.e., the claim of hidden encumbrances, and the like). In addition, this category embraces disputes over the performance of leases as well as suits involving waste, boundaries, manorial rights, and advowsons.

The principal type of *inter vivos* trust litigated relates to marriage settlements; no other type figured frequently.

The single largest sub-category of suits under the heading of debts and bonds, at least for the seventeenth century, involves complainants seeking relief from the enforcement of conditioned bonds and other debt instruments. However, when such credit relationships derived from a sale of goods or other business transaction, the suits have been counted under the heading of business. In other words, the debt/bond category is something of a residual one, including both clearcut cases of financial obligations arising out of personal relationships and also those suits in which the documents simply do not spell out the underlying circumstances. Also included in this category are suits brought by personal creditors of deceased individuals seeking repayment from their legal representatives, and disputes over arrangements involving the transfer of realty or personalty for the benefit of creditors.

---

18 Note that by 4 George II c. 28, sec 3 (1731) on any ejectment, distress, or action for rent, a tenant filing a bill for an injunction for want of an answer from the defendant must verify the material allegations of his bill by affidavit; Fowler, I, 250.

Finally, the grouping labelled business embraces a motley array of situations, among them matters of account between partners or between employers and employees, the sale of goods and services, the collection of business debts (with some plaintiffs in the 1700s assignees in bankruptcy), and occasional insurance and copyright cases. The results of this classification of the sample suits are summed up in Table X.

Table X: Subject-matter of suits in Exchequer samples (excluding tithe cases)

	1685	1735	1785	1819
n =	**96**	**117**	**127**	**132**
	%	%	%	%
Land	32.3	25.6	27.6	26.1
Estate	20.8	20.6	16.9	25.4
Debts and bonds	25.5	22.2	30.3	19.8
Business	9.9	28.2	24.4	24.2
Trust	2.1	0.0	0.0	3.8
Miscellaneous	9.4	3.4	0.8	0.8

All told, the distribution of subject-matter seems both relatively stable over time, with the exception of the greater frequency of business suits from 1735 onwards, by contrast with the declining volume of tithe suits over the period (Table VIII). And, moreover, the balance among the four main types of cases (land, estate, debt, and business) seems relatively constant from 1735 onwards.

By comparison, the Chancery sample data recorded in Table XI below reveal not only a lesser degree of stability over time (note especially the jump in Chancery estate cases in 1785 and the concomitant fall in land cases) but also (a) a consistently lower proportion of debt and business in Chancery than in Exchequer, *and* (b) a higher proportion of land and estate cases in Chancery than in Exchequer. Whereas debt/bond and business cases combined fluctuated in frequency over the four Exchequer samples between 35.4% (1685) and 54.7% (1785) of the respective totals, the frequency of such suits in the four Chancery samples fluctuated between 25.6% (1819) and 36.0% (1685). In other words, by the later eighteenth century – by contrast to a century earlier – there was a wide divergence between the two courts with respect to the frequency of bills of complaint involving disputes over debt/bonds and business matters, and since these, as we shall see, were the topics that most frequently engendered requests for injunctions so 'injunction cases' in Exchequer were extremely common during the later eighteenth and early nineteenth centuries.[19] Again, whereas land and estate suits fluctuated in frequency among the Exchequer samples between 44.5% (1785) and 53.1% (1685), in Chancery such suits fluctuated between 61.2% (1685) and 67.5% (1735).

19 Apart from over-representation of tithe suits (see fn. 10 above) and a marked under-representation of business suits, the frequency of other types of cases among Exchequer reported cases and decrees correspond reasonably well with the levels found in the samples. Business suits amounted to 17.6% of all sample cases, but only 6.5% of printed cases, 8.3% of manuscript cases, and 6.7% of decrees. For these data sets, see Appendix Two.

Table XI: Subject-matter of suits in Chancery samples (excluding tithe cases)

	1685	1735	1785	1819
n =	150	290	140	149
	%	%	%	%
Land	33.1	35.9	20.7	30.8
Estate	28.1	31.6	42.5	32.2
Debts and bonds	18.1	16.0	12.8	9.2
Business	17.9	12.2	17.5	16.4
Trust	2.4	2.9	5.7	10.5
Miscellaneous	0.4	1.4	0.7	0.6

Nor, we may suggest, are the different profiles of Chancery and Exchequer non-tithe business wholly a matter of chance. In the first place, as Table XII illustrates, common injunction requests were much more frequent in debt/bond and business cases than they were in land and estate causes.

Table XII: Frequency of requests for common injunctions in Exchequer by type of suit in four main subject areas (n=693 suits)[20]

Land	42 requests of	168.5 suits	=	24.9%
Estate	20 "	136 "	=	14.7%
Debt/Bond	116 "	195 "	=	59.5%
Business	119 "	193.5 "	=	61.4%

Concomitantly, as suitors increasingly resorted to Exchequer to seek 'common injunctions', so the proportion of debt and bond suits rose in the Exchequer samples (at least up to 1785) while the proportions of such suits in the Chancery samples steadily fell. In the second place, as the Chancery, thanks to the creation of the Accountant-General's office in the mid-1720s, could thereafter offer enhanced security in the supervision of estates of minor beneficiaries, so estate business overtook land matters as the single most frequent type of suit in that court. And the effect of that shift, coupled with the growing proportion of debt/bond suits and business suits in Exchequer, was to generate differences in the speed with which the two courts acted. In 1685, as Table XIII indicates, the rates at which Chancery and Exchequer disposed of suits were reasonably similar. Over the intervening decades, both courts' proceedings were slowed by the tendency of parties (or their legal advisers) to take advantage of the opportunities for delay offered by court process, but in addition, Chancery, with its greater burden of estate

---

20 Data for these four main categories of suits from the four sample sets plus the additional 260 London and Middlesex suits of 1685 and 1785. In addition to the 387 requests for injunctions listed in Table XII, there were also six requests for injunctions in the 133 tithe cases, six in the 10 trust cases, and three in the remaining 24 miscellaneous suits.

administration, fell behind Exchequer. This is evident in measures tabulating all bills filed (Table XIIIa) and in those including only suits that went beyond the pleadings (Table XIIIb).

Table XIIIa: Duration of proceedings in Chancery and Exchequer samples – all bills filed

	Chancery 1685 n=146	Exchequer **1685** n=150	**Chancery 1819** n=149	Exchequer **1819**[21] n=150
Under 1 year	77.4%	78.0%	45.0%	56.7%
1–2 years	12.3%	14.0%	12.1%	16.7%
2–5 years	7.5%	8.0%	25.5%	22.7%
Over 5 years	2.7%	0.0%	17.4%	4.0%

Table XIIIb: Duration of proceedings in Chancery and Exchequer samples for suits that went beyond the pleading stage (measured from time of initiation of suit)[22]

	Chancery 1685 n=35	Exchequer **1685** n=33	**Chancery 1785** n=45	Exchequer **1819** n=29
Under 1 year	40.0%	24.2%	20.0%	13.8%
1–2 years	34.3%	39.4%	20.0%	24.1%
2–5 years	22.9%	36.4%	37.8%	48.3%
Over 5 years	2.8%	0.0%	22.2%	13.8%

(IV) Differences in types of suits and proceedings as between the metropolis and the provinces

As the types of suits entertained in Chancery and Exchequer increasingly diverged, so one can discern an even sharper set of differences in profile as between provincial and London and Middlesex suits initiated in Exchequer. In the first place, the great bulk of tithe suits originated, as we have already observed, in the provinces. In addition, requests for common injunctions were significantly more frequent in London and Middlesex suits than in those from the provinces. This becomes apparent when we consider both the sample suits and the additional 260 London and Middlesex suits drawn from the years 1685 and 1785.

21 Of the six Exchequer cases in the 1819 sample that lasted over five years, three were estate cases. By comparison of the 40 Chancery cases in the 1785 and 1819 samples (combined) that lasted over five years, 28 were estate-related; Horwitz and Polden, 'Continuity or Change', p. 54.

22 No breakdown available for Chancery in 1818/19. For duration of Exchequer suits of the mid-1690s that went beyond the pleadings, see Horwitz, 'Chancery's "Younger Sister"', p. 174, Table VI.

Table XIV: Requests for common injunctions in Exchequer (sample suits and London and Middlesex suits, with tithe suits excluded: n=731)

	1685	1735	1785	1819	Totals
London and Middlesex	43 of 149 28.9%	23 of 44 53.3%	116 of 194 59.8%	35 of 53 67.9%	440 49.3%
Provincial	10 of 63 15.9%	25 of 73 34.2%	24 of 76 31.6%	29 of 79 36.7%	291 30.2%

      Furthermore, it is apparent from Table XV a and b (note cells in bold) that if tithe cases are excluded from the provincial calculations, land suits were far more common among the array of suits emanating from the provinces than among those from London and Middlesex; conversely, business suits were much more common in metropolitan litigation. These differences between the subject-matter of provincial and London and Middlesex litigation were heightened in 1785, as tithe cases declined in frequency, as debt/bond suits declined among cases originating in the provinces, and as estate cases declined among the London and Middlesex suits. Whereas land and estate cases in Exchequer constituted 57.1% of the non-tithe cases from the provinces in 1685, in 1785 their combined total was 65.1%. Again, whereas debts and bonds suits and business suits constituted 42.1% of the London and Middlesex total in Exchequer in 1685, in 1785 their combined total was 67.3%. Thus, the differences detected between the subject matter profiles of the Exchequer and Chancery samples (Tables X and XI, excluding tithe suits) are more or less replicated in the differences apparent in Tables XV a and b as between Exchequer cases (excluding tithes) from the provinces and those from London and Middlesex.

Table XVa: Exchequer 1685 – Subject-matter, London and Middlesex suits v. provincial suits

	London and Middlesex with tithes (n=151)	Provincial with tithes (n=116)	Provincial without tithes (n=63)
	%	%	%
Land	18.5	20.7	**38.1**
Tithes	1.3	45.7	–
Estate	21.2	10.3	19.0
Debts and bonds	21.2	12.1	22.2
Business	**20.9**	3.4	6.3
Trust	2.0	1.7	3.2
Miscellaneous	5.3	6.0	11.2

Table XVb: Exchequer 1785 – Subject-matter, London and Middlesex suits v. provincial suits

	London and Middlesex with tithes (n=194) %	Provincial with tithes (n=99) %	Provincial without tithes (n= 76) %
Land	9.7	32.3	**42.1**
Tithes	2.1	23.2	0.0
Estate	**9.2**	17.7	23.0
Debts and bonds	**34.0**	16.7	21.7
Business	**43.3**	9.1	11.8
Trust	0.0	0.0	0.0
Miscellaneous	1.5	1.0	1.3

Further, since debt/bond and business cases mainly originated from London and Middlesex and since such litigation, whether emanating from town or countryside, produced the most frequent requests for injunctions, it is hardly surprising that requests for common injunctions were much less numerous among provincial suits than among London and Middlesex ones. At the same time, however, it is worth observing that subject type by subject type, provincial suitors were almost as likely as London and Middlesex ones to request injunctions, e.g., 55% of the 40 business suits from the provinces included requests for injunctions as compared with 63.2% of the 153.5 business suits from London and Middlesex. These correlations are illustrated in Table XVI.

Table XVI: Frequency of common injunction suits in Exchequer by subject-matter and geographical origin (n=693)

	Total	Provincial	London and Middlesex
Estate	20 of 136 14.7%	6.5 of 69 9.4%	13.5 of 67 20.1%
Land	42 of 168.5 24.9%	25.5 of 111.5 22.9%	16.5 of 57 28.3%
Debts and bonds	116 of 195 59.5%	32 of 57.5 53.9%	84 of 137.5 61.4%
Business	119 of 193.5 61.4	22 of 40 55.0%	97 of 153.5 63.2%

D. The Valuation of Disputes

It is not possible to put any monetary value on many of the suits litigated in equity in Exchequer (or, for that matter, in Chancery). Above all, the researcher is primarily dependent on the claims of the complainant. And here difficulties arise from two different directions. On the one hand, complainants have an interest in overstating their losses or entitlements. And in the case of relief sought from the enforcement (in other jurisdictions) of penal or conditional bonds, it is also necessary to bear in mind that these instruments were usually made out for twice the value of the underlying transaction (e.g., a £400 bond to secure a £200 or £210 loan).

On the other hand, in many suits, no valuation at all is offered by the parties. This is most commonly the case in suits over estates and land transactions, where the complainant is asking for a valuation of the estate, for the redemption of a mortgage of unspecified value, or for the conveyance of an estate already negotiated.

Thus, what quantitative data that can be derived from the documents may be informative with respect to the individual suit, but are rather less so when it comes to deriving any kind of average. What can be stated without fear of contradiction is that the amounts in question, when alleged, vary from a few pounds to thousands.[23]

Table XVII: Average amount in dispute in suits where a valuation is given

1685 sample (150)	£86 average, 18 cases
1819 sample (150)	£1,251 average, 54 cases

At first sight, Table XVII appears to suggest that not only did the average value of suits rise dramatically between the 1685 and 1819 samples, but that the proportion of suits in which valuations are given also rose substantially. But this impression of change over time is rather clouded by the inclusion of data from the 151 London and Middlesex additional suits for 1685. No less than one-half (74 of 151) of these London and Middlesex disputes are susceptible to valuation, and the average for these suits is £590. Taken together, the two 1685 sets indicate an average valuation of £491 from 92 cases (or roughly 30% of the total 301 cases for 1685). These figures from the two sets of 1685 cases, then, show roughly the same proportion of disputes in which a valuation is stated, with the average valuation for 1685 roughly two-fifths of the 1819 average. But given the wide discrepancy between the results for the two 1685 sets of suits, it seems unwise to place too much faith on either outcome – the comparison of the 1685 sample with the 1819 sample or that of the two 1685 sets with the 1819 sample.

E. The Identity of the Litigants

Having dwelt in so much detail on the differences between London and Middlesex suits on one hand and provincial ones on the other, it might be anticipated that an analysis of the status and occupational profiles of Exchequer plaintiffs would yield similar contrasts. And in some respects this is, indeed, the result. Our approach here has been to focus on the first-named plaintiffs and defendants in the Exchequer suits we have investigated, grouping them in the following categories.[24]

---

23 Tithe suits are a category to themselves, since the owner of the tithes is litigating for an annual sum or payment in kind, and since the often quite small sum found owing by a single defendant may stand as a precedent (or at least a deterrent to resistance) for similarly-situated inhabitants of a whole parish. Moreover, a significant proportion of tithe cases have numerous defendants.

24 Relatively few suits were brought by multiple plaintiffs and of these a significant minority were husband and wife suing together on behalf of the wives' claims (of the 600 sample cases, 127 had multiple plaintiffs; of these 33 were spouses). Many more suits featured multiple defendants, among them suits for tithes and suits against partnerships (of the 600 sample cases, 303 had multiple plaintiffs; of these 47 involved tithe claims). The principal reason for focusing on first-named parties is to avoid the skewing multiple defendants in sizeable numbers (e.g., 15 yeomen in a tithe dispute) would produce in a breakdown of status and occupation. See also Horwitz, *Chancery Equity Records,* pp. 42–3.

(1) 'Gentlemen and above' includes all those who styled themselves as 'gent' and 'esq' in their bills (unless they also provided an occupational designation, e.g. barrister) and all those of higher rank (e.g., knight, baronet, or peer);

(2) 'Commercial and artisanal' includes all those who gave an occupational designation (save for professionals) ranging from banker and merchant to more humble vocations such as wheelmaker;

(3) 'Professional' includes all practising the traditional professions (doctors, lawyers including both branches of the profession, and clergy);

(4) 'Farmers' include all those indicating that they pursued agricultural occupations; besides self-styled farmers, this category embraces yeomen and copyholders, as well as graziers;

(5) 'Women' includes both widows and spinsters, as well as those few married women litigating without being joined with their husbands; the great majority of female first parties were, not surprisingly, widows.[25]

(I) First-named Plaintiffs

In analysing the composition of those individuals named as first plaintiffs, one type of cases – tithe disputes – seemed particularly distinctive because so many of the initiating parties (though not all) were clerics. Thus, the first version of Table XVIII that follows includes tithe disputes; the second version excludes them.

Table XVIIIa: Status/occupation/gender of first-named plaintiffs in Exchequer samples including tithe cases (n=150 in each sample)

	1685 %	1735 %	1785 %	1819 %
Gentlemen and above	24.7	20.7	18.0	32.0
Commercial/artisanal	18.0	34.0	34.0	26.0
Farmers	8.0	10.0	9.3	11.3
Professional	22.7	19.3	18.7	14.7
Women	10.7	8.0	11.3	6.7
Undesignated men[26]	11.3	4.7	8.0	5.3
Minors	1.3	0.0	0.0	0.7
Miscellaneous	0.7	1.3	0.0	0.7
Non-individuals[27]	2.7	2.0	0.7	2.7

25 As most female first plaintiffs were widows (in cases where spouses were litigating jointly the husband is customarily named first), so it comes as no surprise that women plaintiffs, and especially widows, were disproportionately litigating estate-related matters.

26 These individuals did, however, often specify a role, e.g., as a representative of the deceased.

27 Non-individuals include the Attorney-General acting in his official capacity as well as corporate bodies.

Table XVIIIb: Status/occupation/gender of first-named plaintiffs in Exchequer samples excluding tithe cases

	1685 n=96 %	1735 n=117 %	1785 n=127 %	1819 n=132 %
Gentlemen and above	24.0	18.8	18.1	34.8
Commercial/artisanal	27.0	42.7	40.2	29.5
Farmers	6.3	10.3	10.2	12.9
Professionals	**10.4**	**7.7**	**10.2**	**6.6**
Women	14.6	10.3	13.4	7.6
Undesignated men	10.4	6.0	7.9	4.5
Minors	2.1	–	–	0.8
Miscellaneous	1.0	1.7	–	0.8
Non-individuals	4.2	2.6	–	–

However, not all the results of occupational/status analysis displayed in Table XVIIIb are as predictable as the sharp fall in the proportion of professionals (clerics) as first-named plaintiffs once tithe cases are excluded. In particular, the sharp increase in the 1819 sample in genteel plaintiffs and the concomitant decline in commercial/artisanal ones merits notice. Indeed, the percentage of the former is higher in 1819 than in any of the three earlier samples; conversely, the percentage of the latter in 1819 is almost as low as that of 1685. These are counter-intuitive results in the light both of the changing socio-economic configuration of the kingdom and of the long-term rise in the proportion of London and Middlesex suits.[28]

Equally unsettling is the fact that London and Middlesex first-named plaintiffs in the 1819 Exchequer sample are almost as 'genteel' as their provincial counterparts, as demonstrated by Table XIX. While the ratio of commercial/artisanal to gentlemen or above in 1685, 1735, and 1785 is at least three to one among metropolitan plaintiffs, in 1819 that ratio falls to roughly one and one-half to one, even after correction has been made for the substantial number of provincial gentlemen figuring as plaintiffs in London and Middlesex bills in that sample.

28 These results also diverge significantly from those of the Chancery 1819 sample – see Tables 7 and 8 in Horwitz, *Chancery Equity Records*, pp. 42–3.

Table XIX: Leading status/occupation categories of first-named plaintiffs in the four samples (excluding tithe cases but corrected for differences between place of residence of plaintiffs and categorization of bills by county)[29]

	Metropolitan (n=166)						
	1685 (n=33)		**1735** (n=48)		**1785** (n=47)		**1819** (n=38)
Gentlemen and above	3	26.3	6	12.5	9	19.1	**10** **26.3**
Commercial/artisanal	15	45.5	28	58.3	22	46.8	16 42.1
	Provincial (n=298)						
	1685 (n=52)		**1735** (n=69)		**1785** (n=79)		**1819** (n=98)
Gentlemen and above	18	34.6	18	26.1	14	17.7	**37** **37.8**
Commercial/artisanal	10	19.2	22	31.9	24	30.4	23 23.4

(II) First-named Defendants

The two versions of Table XX that follow include and exclude tithe cases, respectively.

Table XXa: Status/occupation/gender of first-named defendants in Exchequer samples including tithe cases (n=150 in each sample)

	1685	1735	1785	1819
	%	%	%	%
Gentlemen and above	20.7	16.7	16.0	10.7
Commercial/artisanal	19.3	23.3	34.7	38.0
Farmers	19.3	14.0	15.3	6.0
Professional	6.7	8.7	2.7	8.7
Women	11.3	10.0	12.7	6.0
Undesignated men	22.0	25.3	18.0	29.3
Miscellaneous	0.0	0.7	0.0	0.7
Non-individuals	0.7	1.3	0.7	0.7

29 In compiling Table XIX, eleven provincial gentlemen figuring as first-named plaintiffs in London and Middlesex bills (nine of them from the 1819 sample – see cells in bold) are here categorized as provincials. The only adjustments needed for all status categories besides those included in this table are (1) one Londoner figuring as a first-named plaintiff in a provincial bill; and (2) two provincial females figuring as first-named plaintiffs in London and Middlesex bills.

Table XX b: Status/occupation/gender of first-named defendants in Exchequer samples excluding tithe cases

	1685 n=96 %	1735 n=117 %	1785 n=127 %	1819 n=132 %
Gentlemen and above	19.8	19.7	14.2	9.1
Commercial/artisanal	26.0	29.1	40.2	43.2
Farmers	6.3	4.3	7.9	2.3
Professionals	7.3	7.7	3.1	8.3
Women	15.6	10.3	14.2	6.1
Undesignated men	24.0	26.5	20.5	29.5
Miscellaneous	0.0	0.9	0.0	0.8
Non-individuals	1.0	1.7	0.0	0.8

(III) First-named Plaintiffs and Defendants compared

In many respects, the trends visible in Tables XX a and b seem predictable either in the light of the trends discernible in Tables XVIII a and b and/or in the light of the changes in case load over the four samples. Thus, the sharp drop in defendants who are farmers parallels the sharp drop in tithe cases. Similarly, the sharp decline in women defendants parallels the decline in women plaintiffs. However, in two important and interlinked aspects, the profiles of first-named defendants differs from those of first-named plaintiffs, especially for the 1819 sample. Whereas the 1819 sample of plaintiffs saw a sharp rise in the proportion of genteel plaintiffs and a significant decline in commercial and artisanal plaintiffs, no such reversal of earlier trends occurs among defendants. For first-named defendants excluding tithe cases (Table XXb), there is rather a new low in genteel defendants and a new high in commercial/artisanal ones. Thus, when we combine in a single table first-named plaintiffs and defendants, the composite picture is, somewhat misleadingly, one of relative stability over time, with the principal longer-term phenomena the substantial increase in commercial/artisanal litigants and the fluctuating proportions of women litigants.

Table XXI: First-named litigants by status/occupation/gender in Exchequer samples excluding tithe cases

	1685 (143) %	1735 (186) %	1785 (218) %	1819 (213) %	Total (760) %
Gentlemen and above (179)	25.9	24.2	18.8	26.3	23.6
Commercial/artisanal (332)	35.0	45.7	46.3	45.1	43.6
Professionals (75)	10.5	2.1	11.5	9.4	9.9
Farmers (68)	8.4	9.1	7.3	10.8	8.9
Women (106)	20.2	13.0	16.1	8.5	13.9

F. Summary and Conclusions

If not all the results of our analysis of Exchequer equity subject-matter and litigants are equally explicable, what should be apparent by now is that the profiles of Exchequer equity suits and the plaintiffs who brought them changed significantly over the two centuries of the Court's operation as a general court of equity. Moreover, these Exchequer profiles diverge in important respects from the profiles of subject-matter and ligitants established in an earlier investigation of Chancery cases from the early seventeeth to early nineteenth centuries.

Of all the noteworthy changes in Exchequer equity business over the period, none is more visible than the sharp decline in the proportion of tithe cases (see Table VIII). And in turn, this decline can be correlated in part with (a) the downturn in the proportion of provincial suits (Table VII), and (b) the rise in the proportion of litigants seeking common injunctions (Table IX).

However, these three developments have different implications for comparisons between the character of equity business in Exchequer and in Chancery, bearing in mind that Chancery's case load was throughout much heavier than Exchequer's and that both courts suffered, though with somewhat different timing, from the massive fall in litigation that spanned much of the eighteenth century (Table III). On the one hand, both courts saw a significant slowdown in the pace at which they processed suits (Tables XIIIa and b). Both, too, saw a rise in the proportion of suits emanating from the expanding London metropolitan area over the period (Table VII), while the decline in tithe disputes litigated in Exchequer made its overall range of business by the later eighteenth and early nineteenth centuries more akin to that of Chancery. But on the other hand, Exchequer equity business became more distinctive over time not only because of the rising proportion of common injunction cases but also by reason of the greater proportion of business and debt/bond suits in Exchequer and the greater proportions of testamentary and land cases in Chancery (Tables X and XI). And in turn, the growing share of testamentary business handled by Chancery appears to have left the Exchequer the speedier of the two equity jurisdictions by the early nineteenth century (Tables XIIIa and b) – a development that may also reflect the much higher proportion of bill-only proceedings in the Exchequer samples and the correspondingly much lower proportion of Exchequer suits that eventuated in decrees (Tables IV, V and VI).

Again, our story is not without its continuities as well as its changes. For one thing, the proportions of women as first-named litigants in the four samples fluctuate but show no trends over time (a result in line with the Chancery data). Then, too, in 1819 as in 1685, most first-named female plaintiffs were widows pursuing either testamentary or land-related claims. In addition, in 1819 as in 1685, the bulk of tithe and land suits were from the provinces, the bulk of business and debt/bond cases from the metropolis, with testamentary suits relatively evenly split between London and Middlesex and the rest of England and Wales. Finally, there is the rise in the already high proportion of commercial/artisanal litigants in Exchequer, numbering nearly one-half of all identifiable first-named plaintiffs and defendants from 1735 onwards.[30]

---

30 Save for the seemingly anomalous social distribution of first-named plaintiffs in the 1819 sample.

CHAPTER THREE
The Records and the Finding Aids

A. The Survival of the Records

Despite the substantial mass of Exchequer equity materials that has survived in the PRO and despite Bryson's confidence that these records 'have survived virtually intact' (whereas other categories of Exchequer materials, and especially those of revenue administration have suffered serious losses and depredations), it would be imprudent to assume the equity side was wholly protected against the usual human failures of the clerical staff, not to mention the occasional 'serious incidents' involving the loss of public records, particularly in the early decades of the nineteenth century.[1]

One indication of the risks of loss and/or misfiling is provided by various heads in the Sworn Clerks' monitory memorandum directed to the underclerks in 1649. Thus, for example, head 18 states that no documents are to leave the Exchequer Office unless duly recorded to 'avoid the frequent [?escaping] of records forth of the office to private attorneys and other places'. Again, head 25 forbids making of copies of keys either to the Exchequer Office or to the record rooms at Westminster and also the copying of any of the stamps appointed for the signing of documents.[2]

Another indication of the partial breakdown in filing of equity materials that seems to have overtaken the Exchequer Office in the eighteenth century is the very existence of series E 216 (Exchequer 'miscellanea B', consisting, before re-arrangement of much of this material, of some 897 bundles, only a portion of them relating to Exchequer equity proceedings). Again, Margaret Condon, in characterizing the various series of so-called clerks' papers (E 218, E 219, E 229, E 230 and E 167), speaks of the 'relative disintegration of a centralized filing system in the late seventeenth and eighteenth centuries'.[3]

However, the process of re-filing has by no means filled all the gaps in the main series of materials. Most seriously deficient, perhaps, are the pleadings in E 112.[4] There are various indicators of the extent of loss and/or misfiling. In the first place, there are, among the main series of E 112, a number of categories of materials which in and of themselves signal loss or misplacement. In the first place, there are the answers without their respective bills. Thus, for William III's reign there are no less than 74 'answers without bills' listed in the bill books for London and Middlesex alone (out of a total of 2,133 sets of pleadings, or 3%); for Anne's reign 131 'answers without bills' for London and Middlesex are listed (out of a total of 2,751,

---

1 Bryson, p. 86 and ff.

2 'Orders to be followed by the Underclerks of the Office of the Remembrancer of the Exchequer', Michaelmas 1649; E 164/61, ff. 88–9 (with the names of the Sworn Clerks, which are lacking in another copy of the 'order' at E 369/118, f.142–4).

3 See her introductory note to E 218 in the Standard List of documents series. And for a contemporary's assessment, note Baron Garrow's observations in Parker v. Everard (1821) in *The English Reports*, vol. 147, 146–7 (Price, IX, 447).

4 By contrast, so far as we can gauge, the various deposition series (principally E 133 and E 134) suffered less from loss or misfiling.

or 4.7%).[5] Secondly, there are, for each reign, the supplementary portfolios containing pleadings out of the normal county sequences.

Besides these internal indicators, there are the situations when a searcher cannot locate the pleadings for suits he/she knows to be in process. Thus, of the 258 suits to come before Chief Baron Ward in the mid-1690s for hearing and decision, the pleadings are missing and/or misfiled in whole or in part for no less than twelve, or roughly 5% of the total.

Nor were the Court's own registers always kept as well as desired. Thus, for example, when the Deputy Remembrancer was sent in Hilary term 1721 to check the records at the Court's request, he had to report back 'that the books were in great confusion and not to be come at.' Consequently, 'the trial was put off till next term.'[6]

Nonetheless, the losses and lack of order in the Exchequer equity records are dwarfed by the documentary problems of Chancery. Similarly, by reason both of its internal organization (which facilitated better record-keeping) and its significantly smaller volume of business, it is easier for the searcher to navigate the Exchequer equity records than the Chancery equity records.[7]

B. The Finding Aids and the Ordering of Documents

(I) On-line Searching and Reference

At the time of writing, the overall state of the finding aids is in flux as the PRO has moved to 'on-line' searching and reference. In the past, the main descriptions of records, and the bodies that generated them, have been the 'Guide' – containing both the 'administrative histories' of individual governmental bodies and a summary listing of all the record 'series' (heretofore, 'classes') – and the 'Standard List' (SL). The latter consists of detailed lists of most series (though some series are still wholly or partially listed only in older, separate non-standard finding aids) providing piece numbers for ordering documents. In addition, many of the lists of individual series in SL are prefaced by introductory notes. The notes for the individual Exchequer equity series are often detailed and were the product of original research done in the course of re-organization of many of those classes (though not E 112, E 133 or E 134) in the early 1980s, supplemented by list revision carried out in the mid-1990s.

Most of the lists are now also available in full on-line in the computerized catalogue of documents and on the web (www.pro.gov.uk). It is therefore possible to carry out key-word searches – a considerable boon, though ultimately the value of such searches is dictated by the quality of the data entered in the computer catalogue. At present, the computer catalogue may contain less detail than the original SL entries for individual pieces in some series (e.g., E 134, E 140) since piece entries, at least for the time being, have been limited to 255 characters.[8]

---

5 IND 1/16834, 16836.

6 Harvard Law Library MS. 1216 (read on fiche), Lightbound v. Russell.

7 Thus, there is only one main series of pleadings in Exchequer and one main set of finding aids to those pleadings; by contrast, in Chancery there are multiple series of pleadings and finding aids to them. See Horwitz, *Chancery Equity Records,* chap. 3.

8 Assurances have been given that these limitations are only temporary.

In addition to the lists, the background material provided by the *Guide* (including the administrative histories of the entities that generated the records) and by the introductory notes to individual series will be available on-line. Nonetheless, it will still be requisite when there is no series list in SL to use the non-standard lists in hard copy, and it may also be relevant for the immediate future to check the original SL version in pursuit of further detail with respect to those pieces whose on-line descriptions have been truncated at 255 characters.

In compiling this description of Exchequer equity series and finding aids to them, I have relied chiefly on SL supplemented by my own researches. Users should be advised that one, and only one, copy of the SL will be kept updated (the so-called 'dark green list set' held in the Research Enquiries Room).[9] Nevertheless, for the foreseeable future, users will need, in a number of important instances, to have recourse to older 'hard copy' non-standard listings of either parts of, or in a few cases, the entirety, of individual series. For these series at least, searches carried out in person at Kew will remain requisite.

(II) *Non-standard Listings and Finding Aids*

Non-standard listings of documents exist in a variety of forms, and those still of value are described below under the relevant series. Many originated as the working records of the officials of the Court themselves; others are the subsequent compilations of PRO staff, genealogists, and scholars. Many, but by no means all, of the non-standard lists are at present shelved *by series number* in the Map and Large Document Room at Kew (hereafter referred to as the Map Room): this is the only open-shelf location for such non-standard lists for the Exchequer equity series. Those not available on the open shelves are kept in the repository and must be called for as documents (particularly those classed as 'IND 1' or as 'OBS 1'). Any difficulties encountered in locating Exchequer equity finding aids not resolved by the 'Finding Aids Location Index' should be put to those of the staff on duty in the Map Room.

Many of the older non-standard finding aids share a number of features:

(1) Most are listings by personal names, rather than by subject matter or by the names of the locales in which the disputes arose;

(2) Most older listings list only the surnames of the first plaintiff and the first defendant – so-called 'alphabets': very important exceptions are the bill books (the listings for E 112; see below under 'Pleadings');

(3) Insofar as these listings are not merely 'alphabets' of parties' names, they tend to be organized by regnal year, and within each year by county.

Given the character of many of these non-standard listings, they have throughout this handbook been referred to either as non-standard lists or as 'alphabets', reserving the term 'index' to identify modern fully-alphabetized listings (whether by name, locale, or subject). Many of the alphabets (some on the open shelves, but others needing to be ordered from the repository) are part of the series 'IND 1' for which a somewhat outdated but still indispensable list exists as Catalogue of Index Volumes (IND. 1) and Obsolete Lists and Indexes (OBS. 1)

---

9 At present, none of the Exchequer lists is in process of revision so that this limitation may not prove to be significant.

(vol. 232 of the 'List & Index Society', 1968). This keys IND 1 volumes to the respective document series to which they relate.10

C. The Exchequer Equity Series and Their Finding Aids (listed here in order of discussion [major series in bold]): E 112, 193, 107, 161, 131, 127, 128 (and after, 162), 125, 133, 134*, 178*, 221, 103, 218, 207, 140, 154, 219, 214*, 192, 194, 195, 162, 130, 126, 159, 101, 164, 165, 167, 185, 204, 217, 222, 225 [total 35].[11] Other related series (all discussed under 'Exhibits'): C 106, C 121*, J 90. Note that some of the above series contain revenue and other non-equity matter as well.

(I) Pleadings

1. E 112 – 2387 portfolios (bundles, etc.) – 1558–1841

This is the main pleadings series for the period covered by this volume (earlier pleadings will be found in E 111). Each portfolio contains anywhere between 20 and 200 sets of pleadings (bills, answers, and related documents). The organization is by reign and by county, e.g., the three portfolios E 112/357–59 contain Bedfordshire pleadings for the reign of Charles II, with each set of pleadings given an individual number within each county sequence. Thus, portfolio 357 contains pleadings 1–60, portfolio 358 contains 61–100, and portfolio 359 contains the remainder of the Bedfordshire pleadings for the reign. (The documents in this series are produced to searchers by the portfolio, a great convenience for searchers interested in particular counties or other specific places; the individual pleadings number is needed to identify the specific suit within the county array.) In addition, and for each reign, E 112 contains, as the final portfolio(s) in each regnal sequence, supplementary pleadings for the reign. These 'supplementary' portfolios contain pleadings not identifiable by county for the reign in question (e.g., for Charles II's reign, the last portfolios E 112/563–69 contain over 1,000 such supplementary items). Finally, the last six portfolios in the entire series, E 112/2382–87, contain undated strays and fragments; spanning the entire period; they are briefly described in SL.[12]

The way into the great bulk of this series is provided by the clerks' bill books, stored in the repository and classified as IND 1/16820–53. These volumes must be ordered up individually. To identify the appropriate book, the introduction to E 112 in SL provides a key linking each bill book to the portfolio of E 112 to which the volume relates.

The bill books are organized in identical fashion to the pleadings themselves – by reign and by county. Within the reign, they are in rough but not exact chronological order, so that some pleadings from the early and middle years of a given reign may be listed only towards the end of the reign.

In searching the bill books, one starts at an advantage if one knows (or at least can make a plausible surmise as to) the county from which the suit emanated. Usually, the suit will be

---

10 A much amended copy is kept at the desk in the Map Room. See also the on-line list (with dedicated terminal in the Map Room) of the PRO's 'Finding Aid Location Index'.

11 Asterisks denote classes not completely listed in the SL.

12 Portfolio 2383 is described as bills and answers of Charles II's reign not entered in the bill books; portfolio 2384 is described as from Court of Great Sessions of Wales, fragments.

listed (and filed) under the county where the disputed property (if tangible) is located (e.g., the bill of complaint of a Londoner claiming tithe rights in a Herefordshire parish would normally be filed under Herefordshire). In cases in which no tangible property was in dispute the most likely county of filing is that of the first plaintiff's place of residence.

The bill books are in a kind of pidgin Latin until the early 1730s[13] (though the pleadings are in English throughout); researchers without much Latin will not find this a serious barrier. First names are usually transmogrified into Latin provided the clerk could think of an appropriate equivalent (e.g., *Johannes* for John, but *Percival* for Percival); last names are more usually left in English. A few examples of entries in Latin (with 'translations') will illustrate the point as well as demonstrate some of the more common abbreviations employed by the clerks. The following instances are taken from the London and Middlesex section of IND 1/16840, f. 164 (part I of the bill books for George II's reign).

Term/Regnal Year   (Number of bill in county sequence) (Parties)

Hi lar[y] p[ri]mo   316   Joh[ann]es Lloyd Cives & Distiller de London Quer[ens] vers[u]s Elizabetham Wills vid[ua] Def[endens]

translated as

Hilary, 1 George II   316   John Lloyd citizen and distiller of London complainant versus Elizabeth Wills widow defendant

or

Pasche p[rim]o   319   Joha[nn]es Radburne de p[ar]och[ia] S[an]c[t]e Axe London ar[miger] et Will[elm]us Beavor de p[ar]och[ia] S[an]c[t]e Margarette West[minster] in com[itato] Midd[lesexie] gen[erosus] & Coghill Knapp de Chalfont St. Giles in com[itato] Bucks gen[erosus] et Eliza ux[or] ejus Quer[entes] vers[u]s Benjamin Hyirmers Jacobum Cavendish ar[miger] co[mmun]iter vocat[ur] D[o]m[i]n[u]m Cavendish Anne et uxor ejus Def[endentes]

translated as

Easter, 1 George II   319   John Radburne of the parish of St Mary Axe, London, esq., and William Beavor of the parish of St. Margaret's, Westminster in the county of Middlesex, gent., and Coghill Knapp of Chalfont St. Giles, Buckinghamshire gent., and Elizabeth his wife, complainants, versus Benjamin Hyirmers, James Cavendish esq commonly styled Lord Cavendish and Anne his wife, defendants

Each successive reign has its own set of bill books, save for William III's reign for which some counties are partially listed, in discrete sections, in the volumes for Anne's reign. In each regnal set the English and Welsh counties are arranged in semi-alphabetical fashion.[14] Given the importance of the finding aids presently kept as IND 1s and given the lack of

---

13 With the exception of the Interregnum years.

14 To complicate matters, the county order in the SL does not follow that of the bill books, e.g., the Welsh counties come first in the bill books, last in SL. Again, Yorkshire is listed under 'Ebor' and hence under 'E' in the bill books but placed under 'Y' in SL.

adequate entries at present in the on-line catalogue, a key to the IND 1s (the bill books) to E112 is provided immediately below:

A key to the bill books (IND 1/16820–16853) to E 112 (taken from the introductory note to that series)

The bill books are generally arranged by reign, and by county within each reign. Entries up to the early 1730s are in Latin, save for the 1650s. For each numbered bill in each county set, the clerks entered the *surnames and forenames* of all plaintiffs and defendants. In addition, for the second half of the seventeenth century and the early years of the eighteenth century, the clerks usually added a brief phrase describing the subject matter of the suit: to give some instances chosen at random (from the bill books for the 1650s) – 'touching 2 bonds of £500 a piece', 'touching the personal estate of . . . Thomas Follibrand'; 'to be relieved against a Bond and action brought in the Common Pleas of the county palatine'.[15]

For most reigns, there are at least two bill books. Those labelled Part I (and sometimes also Part III) start with the Welsh counties and continue through the English counties from Bedfordshire to Monmouthshire (including London and Middlesex as a single grouping and including Yorkshire as 'Ebor'). However, these Part Is (and IIIs) exclude Berkshire, Derbyshire, Dorset, Durham, Hampshire, and Leicestershire; these are listed, along with the rest of the English counties from Norfolk to Worcestershire, in the Part IIs (and sometimes IVs).

Reign(s)	Part		IND 1/
Elizabeth & James I	I		16820
	II		16821
James I	I		16822
	II		16823
Charles I	I		16824
	II		16825
Commonwealth	I		16826
	II		16827
Charles II	I	(12–25 Charles II)	16828
	II	(12–25 Charles II)	16829
	III	(21–36 Charles II)	16830
	IV	(21–36 Charles II)	16831
James II	I		16832
	II		16833
William & Mary	I		16834
	II	(Book I)	16835
William & Mary, & Anne	I		16836
	II	(Book II)	16837
George I	I		16838
	II		16839
George II	I		16840
	II		16841
George III*	I	(Book I)	16842
	II	(Book I)	16843
	I	(Book II)	16844
	II	(Book II)	16845
	I	(Book III)	16846
	II	(Book III)	16847

15 Taken from bill numbers 13–15 for the county of Lancashire; IND 1/16826, f. 191v.

George IV	I	16848
	II	16849
William IV	I	16850
	II	16851
Victoria (to 1841)	I	16852
	II	16853

*Note: the dates of material in Books I to III for George III's reign overlap, with Book I extending to 41 G III, Book II covering 17–60 G III, and book III beginning 20 G III.

As illustrated by the examples above, the individual entries in the bill books usually contain the names, first name as well as surname, of all plaintiffs and defendants involved in the suit.[16] Alongside the parties' names is an indication of the term and regnal year in which the bill was filed and the number within the specific county sequence of the individual file.[17] Occasional marginal notes (of a later date) indicate that a given set of pleadings has been lost or misplaced (i.e., are 'not on the file').[18]

While the bill books do not list items to be found in the 'supplementary' portfolios, there is a separate manuscript listing of these pleadings kept on the open shelves of the Map Room (at E 112, vol. 5); this list is an index by name of parties, both plaintiffs and defendants. It is organized by reign, and within each reign by the surnames of plaintiffs.

As noted above, a check of the bill books and a thorough search of E 112 against the case entries for subsequent stages of suits suggest that some pleadings went unlisted by the clerks and are not to be found in either the county or the supplementary portfolios of E 112.[19]

2. E 193: replications and rejoinders – 10 boxes – Elizabeth I–1842

This class appears to consist in part of strays from E 112 – that is, items originally parts of sets of pleadings in E 112 which, after they became detached, were kept separately. However, items dating from the eighteenth century were probably never kept with the bills and answers to which they relate. The replications and rejoinders are arranged, for the most part, by date, with the entire series consisting of ten pieces (boxes). The documents, as those of E 112, are all in English. For the most part, replications and rejoinders dating after the Court became a general court of equity add little specific factual or argumentative matter to the bill and answer, and by the eighteenth century their filing was a mere formality.

There is a partial index in OBS 1/752; this has to be keyed to the modern list for E 193 in SL. It covers suits only after 1700 and omits many cases.

---

16 It is no small advantage, especially when searching for suits in which the parties bear common surnames, that the Exchequer bill books, unlike most listings of Chancery suits, provide both first and last names of both sets of parties, and also tend to list all the parties to the suit.

17 In searching the bill books, one should bear in mind that a bill may have been filed up to five years, sometimes even more, before the date of the eventual decree (or the date given in a report of the case).

18 Note also the occasional list of 'answers without bills' to be found at the end of certain county entries, e.g., for London and Middlesex for William III's and Anne's reigns. In these instances, it would appear that the bill was never entered on the file.

19 For a glaring example, see the Clegat v. Kinsey suits discussed in Chapter Four.

3. E 107 (appearance books) – 23 pieces – 1588–1841 (for the post-1649 years, there are books for 18 Charles II, 23 Charles II, 12–30 George II, 7–14 George III; thereafter continuous)

These documents (in Latin before 1733) record the appearance of defendants (in response to subpoena or attachment) whether in person or by legal representative, and often indicate whether the appearance is in response to a bill (or to its equivalent, an English information filed by the Attorney-General). Entries are dated sometimes by term, sometimes by day, month, and year. Entries in earlier volumes tend to identify only one defendant; those in later volumes are rather fuller. Even so, not all defendants who answered are listed in the appearance books and, conversely, not all defendants who appeared ever submitted an answer. See also individual clerks' appearance books in E 101, E 140, and E 219.

(II) Minutes and Orders

1. E 161 (the common minute books) – 163 volumes – 1616–1890

Minutes of the Court's proceedings (as distinguished from its judgements or decrees) in both 'English bill' proceedings and revenue cases (in English as well) are kept together in chronologically-organized volumes. No alphabets or other finding aids exist for this series beyond the list of volumes (with their respective dates) in SL. For most of the period under consideration, the making of these minutes was one of the main tasks that fell to the deputy to the King's Remembrancer or to the sworn clerks in the King's Remembrancer's Office. From 1820 to 1841, the duty of taking the minutes was transferred to the newly-created offices of Masters in the Court of Exchequer.

The minutes record motions made in the course of suits (interlocutory matters) and the resultant orders (if any were made), as well as the names of the counsel acting for the parties and also, on occasion, the documents or other proofs read in support of motions. The minutes, then, cover a wide range of matters from the preliminary stages of a suit up to the formulation of a judgement or decree, and also may deal with post-decree matters such as costs and enforcement. Then, too, some orders dealt with the final disposition of suits by way of dismissal, especially if the defendant could persuade the Court that the plaintiff had failed to pursue the litigation within the time-frame set by the Court's rules. Court orders minuted in the volumes of E 161 were subsequently written out on separate small sheets of paper (which survive in E 131, see below) and reviewed for errors by the Barons, counsel, or the clerks themselves, and signed by the clerk in court. Subsequently, the orders were then entered in the registers (which survive in E 127).

Of the three types of documents – minutes, draft orders, and the registers of orders – the fullest are the minutes themselves (as discussed in Chapter One). The most important of matters at least occasionally omitted from E 131 and E 127 concern the Court's proceedings on various pleadings – especially on pleas and demurrers entered by defendants, and also on exceptions to answers entered by the plaintiff. Also noteworthy are the occasional omissions of orders for dismissal of suits without hearing (usually for failure of prosecution by the plaintiff) which are only erratically entered in E 131 or in E 127. Other common omissions concern permission for defendants in the country to answer by commission (customarily coupled with the grant of injunctions to the plaintiff to stay actions against him/her proceeding in other courts until such defendants answered). Thus, there is no substitute in tracing the course of a suit for recourse to the volumes of E 161 although, as discussed below, it may also prove profitable to consult the relevant portions of E 131 and E 127.

2. E 131 (original orders) – 140 boxes – 1660–1842

Not all the original orders survive for these years; occasional terms and even years are missing, and so noted in the series list. Contemporary 'alphabets' survive (IND 1/16860–62, 16867–91) though none is extant for 1660–71 and 1680–86.[20]

Each order included in E 131 has a separate number marked on the document and keyed to the indexes; these numbers are also used (though with some variation) in the volumes of E 127. From Michaelmas 1804, the indexes are alphabetically arranged; prior to that time they are simply in numerical sequence within the term. If the searcher is tracing proceedings in a particular case where the parties' names are known, these indexes may provide a more efficient point of departure than paging through the volumes of minutes in E 161.

3. E 127 (entry books of orders) – 85 volumes – 1661–1841 (and for pre-1661 see E 125 discussed below)

This series lacks volume 29 (covering 10–12 Anne) and several extant volumes have one or more terms missing or only entered in part: such omissions will require recourse to E 131.

All entries are dated and titled with the names of the parties to the suit (in Latin until 1733). Many also indicate whether the action was initiated by English bill (E 112) or was a royal revenue case consequent upon a writ of extent (E 143, E 144, E 202).[21] Each entry is followed by the name or initials of the sworn clerk acting for the party on whose behalf the order was moved and made. The name of counsel moving the order is given in the body of the entry. The primacy of the original orders (E 131) is confirmed by occasional notes indicating the date on which the register entry was made (and showing it followed the date of the order itself).

Because the entries are numbered within each term in accordance with the numbers entered on the original orders, the index volumes for E 131 (IND 1/16860, ff.) can also be employed as a means of locating texts of orders in E 127 for the years from 1689 onwards. However, even in terms where the clerical system was functioning normally, not all original orders in E 131 were entered in E 127: entry required payment of the requisite clerical fees, and not all parties were willing or able to pay.

It should also be observed that certain types of orders frequently appear only in E 127, or only in E 127 and E 131, not in E 161. The most common of such orders involve arranging the Court's calendar, e.g., setting the dates for reading exceptions to answers or for reading pleas and demurrers, as well as setting the dates for the publication of depositions and the

---

20 List & Index Society, volume 232 (pp. 123–4), as well as other finding aids, suggests that these IND 1 volumes are indexes to E 127. Rather, they appear to have been compiled for E 131 – but since the numbering arrrangements for that series are partially duplicated in E 127, these IND 1 volumes can be useful for searching E 127 as well.

21 The records of the revenue business of the Court of Exchequer would repay scrutiny, but this handbook is confined to the equity or 'English bill' jurisdiction.

holding of hearings. These are the so-called 'side bar' orders which were treated merely as matter of administrative convenience and routine.

4. E 128 (original decrees and orders) – 134 files (of which the last five contain undated and/or fragmentary documents) – 1562–1662

Reflecting older clerical practice, original decrees and orders for this period were kept together. The orders in turn were entered in the appropriate volumes of E 125 and, latterly, in the early volumes of E 127.

5. E 125 (entry books of orders) – 39 volumes – 1625–1661

These are the entry books for Charles I's reign and the Interregnum. They are organized in similar fashion to E 127, though lacking the numbering system for entries used in E 127 (and in turn derived from E 131). 'Alphabets' survive at IND 1/16854–60, covering the years from 1631 to 1659 (though with a gap between 1651 and 1658). All entries in E 125 are dated, with each entry followed by the initials or names of the sworn clerks acting for each party. Within each law term, entries appear to be in random order. Most entries lack surname titles, so that the identity of the parties can only be ascertained by a careful reading of the entry itself. There are modern calendars for the reign of Charles I on the open shelves in the Map Room listed under E 123 vols. 9–12; (the heading 'Series III' refers to E 123 items); these volumes list the names of the parties and the county of the suit, but only occasionally do they indicate the subject.

(III) *Depositions and Interrogatories*

1. E 133 ('Barons', i.e., town, interrogatories and depositions) – 12,362 pieces – Elizabeth I–1841 (not in SL, included in computer listing from non-standard listing)

Depositions from witnesses were taken by the litigating parties in the 'proof stage', following completion of the pleadings stage. However, it was possible to proceed to a hearing without deposing witnesses (whether because the suit was a collusive one or open solely to documentary proof).

Witnesses gave their evidence to one of the Barons of the Exchequer (or more commonly to the individual Examiners serving under each Baron) if they lived within a 10 mile radius of the City of London (extended to 15 miles in the nineteenth century). In some suits one encounters both town and country depositions. Depositions were responses under oath to numbered questions (interrogatories) framed by one or other of the parties to the suit. With the Court's permission, a defendant or defendants could be deposed on the basis of interrogatories submitted by the plaintiff. In other words, if parties chose to question either the opposing litigants or witnesses brought forward by the other side, they would have to secure the Court's permission to do so, and the process would require separate interrogatories and generate separate depositions.

Each witness or deponent was identified by the date of the deposition and the names of the parties of the suit. The deponent then supplied his/her name, address, occupation and age.

It was customary to attach the prepared interrogatory to the completed depositions and searchers will find the terms in which the questions are posed in the interrogatories essential to interpreting the deponents' responses.

Depositions were, in principle, to be held in confidence until all examination of witnesses was completed. At that stage, the Court would approve a motion for 'publication' (i.e., making each side's materials available to the other) and also for setting a date for the hearing of the case.

As there is no standard list for E 133, access to the documents from 45 Elizabeth I onwards is via an alphabetical listing by suit title (that is, by plaintiff's surname [Crown revenue cases are listed by defendant's surname]); these 'alphabets' have been keyed into the computer catalogue. By locating the title of the suit in question (e.g., Smith v. Jones), the searcher can identify piece and item numbers and order the documents. Obviously, this is a search procedure that puts a high premium on uncommon surnames, especially since none of the depositions is dated in the 'alphabet' (though the documents themselves are dated!).

2. E 134 ('Depositions taken by commission', i.e., country interrogatories and depositions) – 22,301 pieces – Elizabeth I–1841 (the great bulk of this series is not in SL but has been included in the computer catalogue from the non-standard listings)

Those witnesses who resided outside London and its immediate hinterland were normally deposed by the parties' commissioners at some place convenient to the witnesses' places of residence, though there was nothing in the rules of the Court to prevent a provincial witness from being deposed in town, if that was his preference.

Depositions were taken by commissioners nominated by the parties to the suit but subject to approval by the Court. The procedures followed in taking country depositions (or those taken outside England and Wales) mirror those of town depositions, although complicated by not-infrequent disputes between the parties over the selection of individual commissioners or other administrative arrangements.

During the eighteenth century, the Court made strenuous efforts to assure the accuracy and protect the confidentiality of country depositions: the commissioners and the witnesses signed the depositions, and the commissioners also began to sign the interrogatories when received from the respective parties' solicitors.

There are two sizeable sub-sets of depositions in the series E 134.

a. Main sub-set: 19,609 pieces

Unlike town depositions, the main series of country depositions are reasonably fully listed. A printed calendar covers the years from 1558 to 1760 (*Report of the Deputy Keeper of Public Records,* vols. 38–42). These volumes are shelved under E 134 as vols. 1–5, and their contents have been keyed into the computer catalogue.

For each 'produceable piece', the calendar lists the county, the date of the commission, the date of the depositions, the regnal year and term in which each completed commission was returned to the court, the names of the parties, and (especially important if not always accurate) a description of the subject-matter of the litigation. It should be noted that since the publication of this calendar, some files of depositions dating from the period 1558–1760 have been moved from E 134 to the series of special commissions E 178 (see below). The printed calendar is continued in manuscript in four volumes now shelved in the Map Room alongside the other E 134 lists as vols. 10–13.[22] These list the extant depositions from 1760 to 1841 and now are also on-line.

Readers should bear in mind that the ordering format for the bulk of E 134 requires the use of department code (E), series number (134), and under 'piece/item' the regnal year and abbreviated name of monarch (26Chas2), followed by the law term and then an item number within that term (Mich24). So, this item would be keyed into the computer as E 134/26Chas2/Mich24. [23]

In addition, there is a multi-volume topographical listing derived from the printed calendar for the period 1558 to 1760 (shelved in the Map Room under E 134 as vols. 14–24). These volumes list the depositions by county, and chronologically within each county; and it is in this listing that the files moved from E 134 to E 178 are so noted. In addition, a typescript list of deponents covering the years 1559–1695 is also available in three volumes under E 134 as vols. 29–31. This finding aid, compiled by the genealogist Bernau, divides the country into eight geographical 'regions', each calendared in chronological order with precise references to individual suits. An index to Bernau's compilation (purporting to be both as to parties and as to deponents) is available at the Society of Genealogists' Library[24]; this gives references to the PRO calendars which can then be used to ascertain the piece references by which individual documents can be ordered. However, it would appear that this index has largely been superseded by the on-line searching capacity of the computer catalogue.

b. 'Miscellaneous' series: 2,632 pieces

An additional series of miscellaneous country depositions (formerly E 134 miscellaneous) also exists. These documents (pieces 1–2,362) are calendared in former E 501/9, now vol. 27 under E 134 in the Map Room, and there is a typescript continuation covering pieces 2,363–2,632 which is included in SL. In addition, there is an 'alphabet' of parties and places (now vols. 25–26 under E 134) covering pieces 1–2,362.[25]

The great bulk of this series dates from the reign of Elizabeth I. The ordering format is department letter, series number, 'misc.', and piece number, e.g., E 134/misc/2630.

c. Further supplementary series, E 134/Supp.

A further supplementary series, listed on-line at the very end of the E 134 listing, is designated as E 134/Supp, pieces 1897 to 1906 (that is, 10 pieces consisting of a total of 54 items). (Thus, item no. 3 in supplementary piece 1897 is ordered as E 134/Supp1897/3.) The bulk of these depositions come from the early nineteenth century, but some are earlier and some are only undated fragments.

22 Classified as documents E 501/11–14.

23 Calendar year designations are used during the Interregnum in place of the regnal year format. Note that depositions from the joint reign of William and Mary require a different format than those from the reign of William: E 134/2W&M/Trin2, but E 134/8Wm3/Mich 25.

24 Located in Clerkenwell, London. Access to these and other materials to non-members requires the payment of search fees.

25 Document reference is E 501/7–8.

3. E 178 (special commissions) – 7,379 pieces – Elizabeth I–Victoria (not in SL)

The original PRO list of this series was published in the *List of Special Commissions and Returns in the Exchequer* (Lists & Indexes, vol. 37, 1963); the copy in the Map Room has two sets of addenda at the end as well as additions made to the body of the text. In addition, another small set of addenda in manuscript will be found shelved next to the main list. The list, and the addenda, are organized by county, and then chronologically within the county. (Maps originally filed with other documents in E 178 have, for the most part, been removed and given map references.)

        The commissions in E 178 were commissions of enquiry, primarily in revenue cases but also very occasionally in equity cases; the commissioners were accorded authority by the Court not only to take depositions but also to make judgements. Among the various types of documents comprising the series are inquisitions, surveys, rentals, and depositions. The bulk of them date from 1558 to 1649. They are organized by county and by date within each county.

        See also E 165/45 (commission book 1725–45) and E 204 and E 221 (below).

4. E 221 commission books (for country depositions) – 16 vols – 1573–1841

Largely duplicated by modern listing/indexes to E 134 which were compiled independently; hence, E 221 is chiefly of value when the original records cannot be traced in E 134 (or E 178).

(IV) Affidavits and Related Materials

Affidavits are sworn statements presented to the Court primarily to prove the execution or attempted execution of process, e.g., the service of subpoenas.

1. E 103 (affidavits) – 160 pieces – 1774–1951

Items are identified in the series list by suit title. They are filed by term.

2. E 218 (affidavits, supplementary) – 17 pieces – 1694–1833

Bundles 1–10 (1695–1831) contain equity affidavits as well as revenue affidavits; the remainder are limited to revenue matters. These are unfiled affidavits remaining among the papers of the clerks in court.

3. E 207 ('bille') – 229 pieces – 16 Edward I–14 George III

This class consists of a range of documents held by the King's Remembrancer and the Lord Treasurer's Remembrancer. Among them are affidavits for both revenue and equity causes. Pieces 44–162, deriving from the King's Remembrancer's office, date from 1649 onwards; the pieces are usually divided into separate files by legal term or by groups of terms. Pieces 163–229 ('broken files') are identified by date but not so listed. From 1774, the 'bille' continue as affidavits in E 103.

(V) Exhibits

In addition to the formally designated exhibit series, E 140, this section includes several other Exchequer series containing, at least in part, exhibits, as well as a number of non-Exchequer series which contain Exchequer equity exhibit materials.

1. E 140 (exhibits) – 246 bundles (many with individual items: e.g., bundle one comprises 29 different items) – 1319–1842

This series is organized alphabetically by suit name. The bulk of the exhibits are eighteenth century and early nineteenth century in date. These materials were brought into court for a variety of purposes, sometimes to form part of the instructions for drawing up a bill, sometimes as evidence for the making of reports by the Deputy Remembrancer, and sometimes as direct evidence in support of a party's case. What remains are those documents that parties failed, for one or another reason, to retrieve from the offices of the Exchequer after the termination of litigation. Should the searcher be so fortunate as to locate an exhibit relating to a suit she/he is investigating, the rewards may be substantial, as included among this class are title documents and business papers. The SL also contains a very useful set of 'Supplementary Notes on Exhibits in Particular Suits', which detail the proceedings in some eighteen individual cases. E 140 also include some strays which are not exhibits, some wholly misplaced in this series.

In broad terms, the series is divided into the following main sections:

(a) E 140/1–95: exhibits in suits between party and party, arranged mostly alphabetically by surname of plaintiff or sole named parties;
(b) E 140/96–138: exhibits in Crown causes, arranged alphabetically by surname of defendant;
(c) E 140/139–226: exhibits in unidentified suits, and also papers of the clerks of the Exchequer Office;
(d) E 140/227–46: miscellaneous.

2. E 154 (inventories) – 7 bundles – all pre-1649 save for final items in E 154/7

3. E 219 (clerks' papers) – 715 pieces – 1618–1836

Working papers of the clerks in court in the King's Remembrancer's Office, relating to both equity and revenue causes. They include letters to clerks, drafts and copies of proceedings, and exhibits (including pieces 168–95, 316–60, and 428–679). Cause papers (i.e., subsidiary papers and copies from all stages of a suit) are listed chronologically; there is an alphabetical index by plaintiff's name in SL.

4. E 214 (modern deeds) – 1668 deeds and other evidence of title – 1603–1851 (only Introductory note in SL; included in computer catalogue from non-standard listing)

The series is listed separately with an index of persons, places and ships (shelved not in sequence in the Map Room as E 214, but with other listings of deeds of various series). Deeds listed are mainly from the first half of the seventeenth century, but a substantial minority date from 1660. It should be noted that the documents include a significant number of agreements, contracts and bonds of various types, including some relating to commercial activity and some concerning decedents' estates.

5. E 192 (Private papers and exhibits) – 29 pieces – 1527–1829

Included are stray but voluminous exhibits as well as the papers of Baron Ward and his examiners.

6. C 106 (Chancery: Master Richards' Exhibits – 239 pieces – Henry III–1853

When the equity jurisdiction of Exchequer was merged into that of Chancery in 1841, some Exchequer exhibits from ongoing cases were transferred to Chancery as well and now reside in C 106. The SL contains a piece by piece description but it does not identify the materials by the court in which the litigation occurred.

7. C 121 (Chancery: Master Richards' Documents) – 457 pieces – c.1600–1900 (not in SL)

The only finding aids are IND 1/6626–27 (these must be ordered as documents from the repository): these are separate alphabetical suit listings with references that do not necessarily produce the correct documents. Given this situation, this series is perhaps of more use for generic searches than for locating material relating to a specific suit.

8. J 90 (Supreme Court of Judicature and former Superior Courts): documents exhibited or deposited in court) – 2,100 pieces – c.1700–1953

These records are listed in rough date order by suit title (when known) in SL which also contains indexes of persons, places, subjects, and suit titles. Most of the pre-twentieth century exhibits apparently derived from Chancery cases but some derived from Exchequer equity suits. Exchequer material can only be located by reference to suit titles. Note that SL gives more detail about each piece than does the listing on the computer catalogue. In particular, SL notes for many exhibits the date of the relevant order in Chancery, thus helping to distinguish exhibits originating in Chancery from those originating in Exchequer or in other courts such as King's Bench.

(VI) Reports and Certificates

1. E 194 (reports and certificates) – 112 pieces – 1648–1841

These documents, which relate both to substantive issues of fact referred to the Deputy Remembrancer (and later the Master of the Reports) and to issues of costs, are organized on a year by year (and within each year, term by term) basis. Alphabets by suit name exist at IND 1/16892–96. The documents usually indicate the suit to which they are related, and the date of the Court's order of reference of the matter.

2. E 195 (miscellaneous reports) – 9 pieces – 1630–1841

This series includes occasional substantive reports, but most of the documents are either Bank of England certificates of payments made or parties' exceptions to reports.

(VII) Decrees

Decrees were the sentence or order of the court made after full hearing. They were founded on the minutes of the hearing. These minutes, before 1695, were entered on the lists made for the benefit of the Barons of the causes to be heard, day by day. Such lists survive from Michaelmas 1595 through Trinity 1688 as 'bills of causes with minutes' in E 162/48–88. Thereafter, beginning in 1695 there survives a separate series of minute books as E 162/1–46.

1. E 162–89 volumes and bundles – 1595–1841

a. E 162/1–46 – 1695–1841
This continuous series of minute books were at one time known as the 'Exchequer Chamber' minute books – a reference to the inner chamber of the Court of Exchequer in which causes were heard and in which decrees (and some orders) were made in consequence of such hearings. Most of the decrees were then filed in E 128 and E 130 and entered in E 126, but some were never filed or entered. The minutes were taken by the Deputy Remembrancer, or by one of the sworn clerks in the King's Remembrancer's Office. In 1820, the task was transferred to the newly created offices of Masters in the Court of Exchequer. There is no index to these materials.

The minutes usually list the names of the Barons present, as well as of counsel appearing. They also summarize the evidence presented by the opposing sides, objections to the evidence and the decisions on such objections, and the decree or order made by the court.

b. E 162/48–88 – Michaelmas 1595–Trinity 1688, but with many terms and some years missing
From 1595 onwards, minutes of court action were entered on the bill of causes for a given day of hearing. In form, they consist of the list of individual causes to be heard, with spaces left between the title of the suits in which the Deputy Remembrancer could subsequently enter the outcomes, if any. The amount of information minuted for any given suit varies considerably. Such bills of causes with minutes survive for a span of post-1695 terms (1695–1710) in the papers of Chief Baron Edward Ward in Lincoln's Inn Library; like the documents in E 162/48–88, the Ward bills of causes contain notes of outcomes. In addition, some of the Ward documents include notes of depositions read and counsels' arguments.

c. E 162/47 and 89
These are papers of causes *without minutes* for 1584–1602 and for 1704–58.

2. E 128 (original decrees and orders) – 134 files – 1562–1663

Reflecting older clerical practice, original decrees and orders for this period were kept together. In 1605, the decrees began to be entered in the appropriate volumes of E 126 and then in E 130.

3. E 130 (original and copy decrees) – 75 boxes – 1660–1841

This series of original decrees is continued from E 128. From the 1670s, each original decree is numbered and the class has a detailed set of alphabets (IND 1/16862–68, listed in List & Index Society vol. 232 under E 126) running continuously from 1677. These are arranged by year and term, and give for each suit the surnames of the first named plaintiff and defendant, listed in numerical order of the decrees, and then (save between 1728 and 1737) the folio of the entry book of E 130 in which the particular decree was entered.[26]

4. E 126 (entry book of decrees) – 57 volumes – 1605–1841

For these entry books, the most convenient means of reference are the modern calendars for the years 1605–93 (these are shelved in the Map Room under E 126 as vols. 1–4). They provide for each decree in the relevant years of E 126 the folio of the entry, the date of the decree and order, and the parties' names. Moreover, they give an indication of the subject matter of the suit or the substance of the decree. For the subsequent years, the alphabets in IND 1/16862–68 (as described under E 130) are available.

The E 126 volumes themselves are organized term by term, and the decrees are given in full, usually with the name(s) of the presiding Baron(s).

5. E 159 (King's Remembrancer memoranda rolls) – 789 rolls – 1218–1926

As the careful introductory note in SL to E 159 explains, the Court's equity business has only a minor place in the diverse matters recorded on these rolls. Enrolment of decrees was not the norm in the Court, even in the seventeenth century, and enrolment becomes increasingly uncommon thereafter. However, there is one brief interval when decrees are not entered in E 126 but only in E 159 – the period from Michaelmas 1673 to Hilary 1675. The precise reason for this departure from normal practice is unknown though one may infer a dispute over fees; in any event, there is no other instance of such deviation from usual practice in the treatment of decrees.

It would appear that the chief reason for a party to undertake the extra expense of enrolment was to make life more difficult for a determined opponent. A decree could be petitioned against by the losing party who needed only to make a prima facie case in order to secure a rehearing by the Court. Once enrolled, however, the victor's opponent would have to go by way of a bill of review, a more costly and apparently more difficult course. However, the norm was that only a fraction of the decrees promulgated by the Court were enrolled in E 159 (see Table II, p. 33).

Locating the decrees that were enrolled in the volumes of E 159 is possible via the

---

26 See also fn. 12, Chapter Four.

so-called agenda books beginning in Henry VIII's reign – IND 1/17051–79 (36 Henry VIII–46 George III) and continued in IND 1/6724–32 (Easter 1806–Mich. 1884). There is also the roughly parallel series of repertory rolls but these cease in the later seventeenth century – IND 1/7031–51 (1 Edw I–32 Chas II, but with 6–11 Chas I and 16–27 Chas II wanting). Both the agenda books and repertory rolls must be ordered from the repository.

In addition, some enrolled decrees can be located using Adam Martin's *Index to Various Repertories, Books of Orders, and Decrees, and other Records Preserved in the Court of Exchequer* (1819). Martin, who served for over 60 years first as a side clerk and then as a sworn clerk (1720–52, 1752–83), provides references to the repertory rolls from 1272 to 1649 and the agenda books from 1649 to 1760. Entries are arranged alphabetically according to the name of the place or property in question. Using Martin's *Index* (available in the Map Room), then, it is possible to move directly from his entries to the rolls, as well as to the Court's decree and order books from 1558 to 1774. However, it should be borne in mind that the *Index* merely selects from the PRO series to which it refers and its entries must be keyed to modern series lists.

Another version of Martin's index to the E 159 rolls and to the decree books was published in 1794 by Hutton Wood. This listing (IND 1/17050) notes the decrees and enrolments by county and then chronologically within each county. Hutton Wood's volume is, apparently, an earlier revision by David Burton Fowler of Martin's work, which does extend somewhat the chronological span of Martin.

It would appear, then, that the searcher would have need to have recourse to E 159 to locate the text of a decree only in those unusual circumstances in which a decree (known to or believed to exist) cannot be traced in E 126, E 128, or E 130.

(VIII) Ancillary Matters

1. E 101 (accounts, various)

Among the later accessions to this sizeable series are several clerks' books of account, especially E 101/637/8, E 101/638/1, E 101/638/5. In addition, there is an appearance book covering the years 1778–1784 at E 101/638/4. A list of these later accessions to E 101 is printed as *Supplementary Lists of Accounts, Various of the Exchequer (*List and Index Supplements, vol. IX, no. 1, 1969); a copy is shelved in the Map Room.

2. E 164 (miscellaneous books, a number of which really amount to exhibits), series 1 72 pieces – temp. Edward I–mid-19th century

3. E 165 (miscellaneous books, series II) – 163 pieces – c.1488–1989

As the title indicates, this is a portmanteau class which contains writ and commission books, as well as an imperfect account book of funds in court. See also E 204.

4. E 167 (papers of the clerk to the Deputy Remembrancer) – 87 pieces – 18th–early 19th centuries

Miscellaneous material relating to the conduct of the Office of the Exchequer, especially concerning fees.

5. E 185 (petitions) – 17 bundles – 1627–1841

Numbers 1–15 contain miscellaneous equity and revenue petitions, 1800–41.
Numbers 16–17 consist of petitions for admission as a pauper (*in forma pauperis*), 1627–1796 (and one 1840) in date order, and 1712–26 (not in date order).

6. E 204 (entry books of writs, commissions and injunctions) – 14 volumes – 12 George I–1842 (vol. for 1790–96 missing)

Earlier books of the same type are to be found in E 165. Included are both revenue and equity matters. Most entries give some indication of the payment of fees, or of admission *in forma pauperis*.

7. E 217 (account books, ledgers, and dividend books concerning funds paid into Court and administered by the Court) – 131 volumes – 1675–1841

Volume 131 is a register of money paid into and out of court, 1675–1725, and of writings delivered into and out of court, 1707–13 (see also E 165/146 accounts of funds in Court, 1785–1871).

8. E 219 (clerks' papers, see also under Exhibits) – 720 bundles – 1625–1841

Includes briefs and cause papers, as well as exhibits, and much matter relating to the conduct of equity business.

9. E 222 (subpoena book of 1667–70 – the only surviving); see also E 219/684 – clerk's subpoena book for 1730

10. E 225 (Registrar's accounts for decrees and orders) – 7 volumes – 1726–97

Accounts, by term and by the appropriate clerk in court, of the fees for entry and for copies of decrees and orders, kept by the Register of decrees and orders.

CHAPTER FOUR
Searching the Exchequer Equity Records

This chapter offers some advice on how to go about searching the records. The first section provides a brief account of how some previous searchers have proceeded and succeeded in terms of three distinguishable types of searches: for information about a particular place, about a particular individual, and about a particular subject. The second section offers some general suggestions about exploiting the better finding aids available for several of the more important classes. The third section is intended to illustrate, by means of 'specimen' searches (chosen in part to reveal the range of materials that can be found and in part to illustrate the limitations and complexities of the finding aids), how to begin to grapple with the records of Exchequer equity proceedings. This third section concentrates on searches about particular individuals and specific subjects.

A. Some Successful Searches

(I) About particular places

One major historical/topographical project has made extensive use of Exchequer equity materials – the postwar segment of the 'Victoria County History of England'; the classes most used have been E 133 and 134 followed by E 126 (decrees). Paradoxically, E 112, the main series of pleadings, even though organized by county (within each reign) and produced to readers as entire portfolios, appears to have been rather less used.[1] The pleadings have, however, been extensively drawn upon by several scholars (notably John Broad and Richard W. Hoyle) in a recent collective history of Bernwood Forest, Buckinghamshire; all told, they were able to locate some 25 sets of pleadings relevant to their enquiries, along with 15 sets of depositions from E 134 and three other sets of commissions of inquiry and returns in E 178.[2] Another recent example of the systematic 'mining' of Exchequer equity records (primarily E 134, depositions taken in the provinces) to illumine the history of a particular socio-economic milieux is Andy Wood's study of the lead-miners and the lead-mining industry of the Derbyshire Peak Country in the early modern period. All told, Wood was able to locate no less than 3,779 depositions, spanning the period 1519–1754, taken by commission in the Courts of the Duchy of Lancaster and of Exchequer and relating to litigation from the heartland of the Derbyshire lead industry.[3]

---

1 Whereas Chancery pleadings are produced on a case by case basis (i.e., singly), the whole portfolio in which a given Exchequer pleading is stored is produced for the searcher.
2 *Bernwood Life and After-Life of a Forest*, John Broad and Richard W. Hoyle, eds. (Preston, 1997), pp. 19–107.
3 Andy Wood, *The Politics of Social Conflict: The Peak Country 1520–1770* (Cambridge, 1999), pp. 130–2, 328.

(II) About particular persons and particular subjects

Searches for particular individuals have been the most common way to try to make use of Exchequer equity materials, in part by reason of researchers' interests but also in part because of the limited possibilities for direct subject searching (confined chiefly to the calendars to E 126 and E 134). In other words, investigators seeking to extend their knowledge of a specific subject have often had to fall back on searching for suits that involved individuals related to the subject in question. This is particularly true for searches beginning with Exchequer equity pleadings as filed in E 112 (by reign, and within each reign by county) and listed in the clerks' bill books. Thus, it will make sense to discuss searches for individuals and for subjects in conjunction.

Searches of the bill books with a list of relevant individual names is undoubtedly tedious but can be highly profitable. One good instance is that of the economic historian Jacob Price as illustrated in the researches for his article 'Sheffield v. Starke: Institutional Experimentation in the London–Maryland trade c.1696–1706'. Much of his evidence for this study derives from the documents generated by a long-running dispute between a London merchant, Thomas Starke, and his former apprentice and Maryland agent, John Sheffield. All told, Price draws upon nine different series of Exchequer equity records (as well as other extant records in the PRO and in the Maryland archives) to document his account of the conduct of Sheffield's business – 'the earliest known records of a British firm trading to the Chesapeake' – and to support his analysis of the early phases of Anglo-American trade in that region.[4]

The researches of Judith Milhous and Robert Hume, the theatre and opera historians, also demonstrate the quality and quantity of materials to be found in Exchequer equity records. Searching for the name 'William Sheldon' (a key backer of the Pantheon opera project) in later eighteenth-century London), Milhous and Hume were able to locate in E 112 via the bill books four separate suits in which he was a party and in which material relating to the building was central. Two features of the bill books, in particular, facilitated their searches:

(1) that, given their subject, they needed only to search the London and Middlesex portions of the books for the relevant time span; and

(2) that the bill books usually list the parties by their forenames as well as their surnames. All told, in addition to the four Sheldon suits, Milhous and Hume were able to locate no less than 20 other Exchequer cases 'relevant to our book'.[5]

Another instance of subject searching by name takes advantage of the bill books' identification of female litigants by the device of supplying parties' first names. With this information, it is possible to summon up suits of female plaintiffs which yield significant

4 *Business History* 18 (1986), 19–39 at 34.
5 Milhous and Hume, 'Eighteenth-century Equity Lawsuits', p. 239 (they also found a substantial number of Chancery suits related to their topic). Note also the ongoing work of Professor Nancy A. Mace on music copyright and related topics as, for instance, 'Haydn and the London Music Sellers: Forster v. Longman & Broderip', *Music & Letters* 77 (1996), 527–41.

information on various topics relating to gender. A particularly assiduous exponent of this technique has been the social historian Margaret Hunt, who has concentrated on women plaintiffs appearing in the London and Middlesex sections of the bill books for the later seventeenth and early eighteenth centuries; in addition, she has made use of women's petitions to file in forma pauperis in E 185. Drawing upon the detailed accounts of their circumstances alleged by the plaintiffs (many of them domestic servants, sailors' wives, and other relatively poor women), she has produced a number of studies illuminating female attitudes towards work and the remuneration of work. In all, her enquiries have yielded over 760 Exchequer equity cases from 1700 to 1720 (the bulk of them from London), and from her samples she estimates that perhaps as many as 15,000 women figured as parties in Exchequer equity proceedings of the eighteenth century.6

B. Suggested Search Procedures

(I) For places

Although most of the finding aids consist of lists of (parties') names, it is possible to secure entry to various of the Exchequer equity materials by listing of or at least by mention of place in the appropriate finding aids.

One might instance here three different routes into the documents. The first would be via the bill books to E 112. As we have noted in Chapter Three, the bill books specify place for a large number of suits for the second half of the seventeenth century and into the early eighteenth century; however, later they supply place names only occasionally. Nonetheless, these place names are sometimes difficult to comprehend, as up to the early 1730s most (save for the 1650s) are rendered in Latin.

Suppose, then, that one was interested in the Devon town (parish, hundred, and manor) of Ottery St. Mary in the period 1650–1760. One could, by searching the Devonshire sections of the bill books covering these years, expect to identify most, if not all, the suits involving Ottery St. Mary parties or issues during the period in question.

An alternate route, particularly useful for those periods where the bill books are not very rich in place names, would be for the searcher to start with the entries for E 134 (depositions taken by commission) in the computer catalogue. These documents can be searched in a variety of ways, including by place name. It is, then, relatively straightforward to use the computer catalogue to identify Exchequer equity suits connected with a given place (or its inhabitants) – for instance, Ottery St. Mary. To be sure, because the index covers only suits that reached the proofs stage (depositions), one could not in this fashion identify suits that failed to get beyond the pleadings. Even so, if the search covered, say, a century, one would

---

6 Margaret Hunt, unpublished papers: 'Women and Money: female litigants in equity in eighteenth-century England'; 'Women, Credit, and the Seafaring Community in early eighteenth-century London'. See also M. Hunt, 'Marital Strife and Female Resistance in the London Courts in the early Eighteenth Century', *Londinopolis,* Mark Jenner and Paul Griffiths, eds. (Manchester University Press, forthcoming). Compare Hunt's estimates of the number and proportion of female litigants (c. 40%) with our data in Tables XVIIIa and b, pp. 48–9, for the proportions of first-named female *plaintiffs* (roughly 10% or less of all plaintiffs).

expect to come up with at least a few sets of depositions related to the village's affairs and/or inhabitants.[7] And once identified in this fashion, one could locate the suits in the relevant bill books, read the pleadings, and follow these cases through the other relevant Exchequer equity classes. One might also profit from collecting the names of individuals involved in these suits to serve as a search list in further enquiries.

A third possible route is via the calendars of decrees (E 126) covering the years 1605–1693 (shelved in the Map Room under E 126, vols. 1–4). As the calendars provide an indication of the subject matter of the suit or the substance of the decree, it should be possible thereby to identify all Ottery St. Mary cases for the years in question that reached the decree stage (and in like fashion as above) to locate the pleadings and other relevant pre-decree material for these suits. Withal, it must be said that provided the searcher began with or could accumulate in the course of initial searches a substantial list of names of inhabitants of Ottery St. Mary, he/she might be well advised to concentrate thereafter on searching the Devonshire segments of the bill books for these named persons, rather than pursuing any (or all in combination) of the above-described searches by place.

(II) For subjects

As noted above, the bill books, at least for the later seventeenth and early eighteenth centuries, the calendars for E 126, and the listings for provincial depositions (E 134) can all be searched with profit for information on subject matter, as well as on place.

C. Specimen Searches

Here, the aim is to 'walk through' a variety of separate searches for cases ranging from the mid-1600s to the early 1800s, partly to illustrate the character of the relevant finding aids and partly to draw attention to the different kinds of material beyond the pleadings that may survive. In most of the examples, the surnames of the principal plaintiff(s) and defendant(s) are assumed to be known at the outset.

(I) Biss v. Biss, 1685–c.1688, payment of a bond

Let us begin with a relatively straightforward case – a suit traceable through at least seven series of Exchequer equity materials. The plaintiff, the widow Elianor Biss of Wells, Somerset, was seeking payment of a bond issued to her late husband George Biss esq. by his late brother Edward Biss esq. of Batcombe, Somerset as a security for sums owing. The defendants were her nephew James Biss esq. (son of the aforementioned Edward) and the parish incumbent of Batcombe, Somerset, Thomas Holt DD (the actual holder of the bond and apparently acting as a sort of third-party stakeholder).

The pleadings file, located (via the bill books) in the portfolio E 112/603, contains a

---

7 In fact, carrying out this search yielded nine sets of depositions related to Ottery St. Mary for the period under examination. Not surprisingly, E 134 was rather more profitable than E 133 in this instance.

number of documents. First, there is the bill itself, numbered as Somerset 56 (of this reign), and filed in Easter term 1685, the first year of James II's reign. In addition, since both defendants chose to answer in the country, there are included in the same file 56 the two commissions to take their respective answers, two copy bills to accompany the commissions, and finally, there are the texts of Holt's answer, sworn as of 20 June 1685, and of James Biss's, sworn as of 27 October 1685.

The proofs stage in this suit consists simply of the taking of sworn statements of witnesses by both sides. The commission for taking depositions from the parties' witnesses is dated 28 November 1685 and is part of the file identified as E 134/1&2Jas2/Hil18.[8] The depositions themselves were taken at Wells, Somerset on 25 January 1686, and, along with the interrogatories to which the deponents were responding, form the rest of the E 134 file. All told, some seven individuals were deposed, four solely for the plaintiff and three for both parties. For the plaintiff, the deponents were four middle-aged landed gentlemen, for the rest they included a local yeoman, a local clothier, and another local landed gentleman. Testimony focused on the circumstances of the issuance of the bond and whether or not repayment had been made either in full or in part.

Subsequently, a court order of 5 February 1686 (E 131/5/3, no. 62) was made stipulating the 'publication' of the depositions and arranging for a hearing of the case during the succeeding term.[9] The hearing came on on 18 May 1686, and at this juncture the plaintiff accepted a compromise offer from her nephew – to pay within a year £300 and interest on the bond. This compromise was embodied in a decretal order (E 126/14, f. 396, located using the modern calendars shelved in the Map Room).[10]

Unfortunately, the implementation of the order did not go smoothly. In November 1687, the plaintiff was back before the Court getting an attachment authorized and issued against her nephew for his failure to pay (E 161/50, f. 81v).[11] Even so, the plaintiff was, as it were, compelled to pursue her nephew from beyond the grave, as in late October 1688, the plaintiff's executrix was moving the court to revive and to enforce the original order of 1686. No further process in the case has been traced, so we cannot be sure whether the defendant was at last compelled to implement the agreement he had made with his deceased aunt two and one-half years earlier (E 131/5/4, no. 14).[12]

---

8 The file was located by searching the on-line catalogue which incorporates the printed calendar to this series. It could also have been located by searching the printed listings.

9 Note that the alphabet for this year is missing; the order was located by searching the relevant 'piece' of E 131. There is a parallel entry in E 127/15. And see fn. 12, below.

10 No enrolment appears on E 159.

11 Located by date in E 161/50. There is a parallel entry in E 127/16.

12 There is a parallel entry in E 161. It should be noted that although there are no indexes to the Court's orders, as recorded in the 'Common Minute Books' (E 161), there are alphabets for the 'original' orders (individual slips in E 131) and these E 131 alphabets can also be used to search the 'entry book' of orders (organized by term) in E 127 as explained in Chapter Three above under E 131 and E 127. As for the decree series, there is, in addition to the modern calendar to part of E 126, a series of 'alphabets' which cover the rest; these also serve as 'alphabets' to the 'original decrees' in E 130, and, indeed probably were compiled from E 130 rather than E 126. No alphabet or other finding aid exists for the decree books or for the 'Exchequer Chamber minute books' of E 162 (a series beginning only in 1695).

(II) Hole v. Greenslade, 1819–21, payment of a promissory note

While Biss v. Biss is unusual among the cases of the 1685 sample in that the litigation was carried through the proofs stage and eventuated in a decretal order, it nonetheless consumed only six terms (not counting the post-decree proceedings of 1687–8). A contrasting case taken from the 1819 sample, Hole v. Greenslade, illustrates the longer length and greater procedural complexity of many later cases. The case featured Robert Hole, gentleman of Timberscombe, Somerset, and his fellow plaintiff Joan Ridler of Porlock, Somerset; they were seeking payment of promissory notes that the defendant John Greenslade, yeoman of Minehead, Somerset, had issued to them in return for loans. A second defendant subsequently emerged, one Philip Hancock, gentleman of Wiveliscombe, Somerset; he had recovered a verdict in Exchequer equity against Greenslade and now occupied Greenslade's premises.

The original bill of complaint was filed in Michaelmas 1818 (being numbered Somerset 1156 for the reign of George III), and this file, E 112/1953, no. 1156, was enlarged by a supplemental bill dated 21 June 1819 in order to bring the additional defendant, Hancock, into the proceedings. Also included in the pleadings file was a commission for taking Hancock's answer in the country, as well as Hancock's answer of 12 November 1819 responding to both the original and supplemental bills. So already four terms had passed, and although Greenslade had been served with a subpoena to appear (affidavit of 19 January 1819 in E 103/37, unfoliated, bundled by term) and had in fact appeared in Easter term (E 107/16, unfoliated, organized by term), he had yet to answer.

In fact, Greenslade's appearance in Easter term 1819 was the last the Court was to see or to hear of him. While Hole responded to Hancock's answer with a replication in Easter term 1820, and proceedings were undertaken to put Greenslade's property into receivership beginning in October 1819 and culminating the following May (E 103/40, E 218/17 [affidavit of 24 May], E 194/70 [no. 94, certificate of appointment of 31 May in a bundle partly organized by letter of the alphabet]), Greenslade never submitted an answer either to Hole's original bill or to his supplementary bill. Finally in late December 1820, after a commission of rebellion directed to a group of Somerset men had failed to bring Greenslade to heel, the plaintiffs secured an order for the Court's Serjeant at Arms to arrest him (E 161/140, unfoliated, 16 Dec.), E 131/80 and E 127/63 (both no. 246). However, even this intensification of the contempt process failed to secure Greenslade, and the case was dismissed without a hearing on 10 May 1821 (E161/140, E 131/81 and E 127/63) after the plaintiff chose to proceed no further against Hancock.

Yet if Hole and Ridler would appear to have been frustrated by Greenslade's disappearance, they could probably console themselves with the proceeds they were in receipt of once Hancock had been replaced on Greenslade's premises with a Court-appointed receiver seemingly of their choice, one John White gent. of Stogumbeer, Somerset (for whom sureties were furnished by Robert Hole the younger and James White gents). All told, then, these proceedings consumed eleven terms, without ever having gone beyond the complications of the pleading stage, in part because of the disappearance of the principal defendant.

(III) Crane v. Hill et al., 1693–5, title to a rectory

A rather different procedure for searching is required when one begins *in medias res* – a situation that might, for instance, arise by having found some documentation relevant to an Exchequer equity suit in a family manuscript collection, and wishing to uncover the substance and full course of the suit. Here we draw upon the material related to suits heard by Sir Edward Ward during his tenure as Chief Baron of the Court from 1695 to 1713 and preserved among his papers in Lincoln's Inn Library. One such case is Crane v. Hill which was heard by the Court in late 1695.

The plaintiff was William Crane, and he was suing John Hill and three others in a dispute over title to the rectory of the parish church of Hales, Suffolk. We first encounter the suit in Ward's papers in late June 1695, when it was one of a number being scheduled for hearing the following term (Michaelmas); we subsequently encounter it at the hearing stage in late November and early December 1695.[13]

From Ward's notes of the proceedings we learn that the original transaction went back to the mid-1670s and that in the early 1680s the dispute had been litigated in Chancery in the suit of Hill v. Crane, a suit which had gone at least as far as the proofs stage. Crane now wanted to use depositions taken in that Chancery suit in the current Exchequer litigation, but his efforts to have them accepted were being opposed by Hill. The acceptability of these depositions was debated when the hearing was scheduled in June 1695, and again at the hearing itself late in the following term. Initially the Barons refused to allow their use on the grounds that there was no bill and answer extant from the Chancery proceedings (i.e., there were no pleadings to put the depositions in context); subsequently, in December the depositions were allowed in as evidence for Crane because he now produced the 'original of bill and answer' from the Chancery suit.[14]

At this hearing, the Court, having reviewed the evidence as presented by opposing counsel, ruled for the plaintiff. Ward noted the facts of the dispute and the grounds of his opinion in favour of Crane (not given in the official Exchequer decree).

The land in question was part of a purchase made by the plaintiff from the defendant in 1675 when the defendant succeeded his heavily-indebted father. By the terms of the transaction, the plaintiff was to discharge Hill's father's debts to Crane and also to pay the defendant an agreed annual sum as maintenance, for the defendant's life. Subsequently, in 1682–3 Hill initiated a suit in Chancery seeking to set aside the bargain in part (with respect to the rectory of Hales). However, Hill's bill in Chancery was dismissed upon hearing (though that order of dismissal was not drawn up and entered). Hill later turned to the common law, and in an action of ejectment at the summer assizes of 1693 at Norwich succeeded in having Crane removed from possession of the rectory on the grounds that despite the conveyance of 1675, he still possessed a superior claim at law that came independently of his father from his

13 Lincoln's Inn MSS Misc. 515, f. 7; and 514, ff. 42, 43–4.

14 In the event, Ward records that the Barons divided three to one in favour of allowing the depositions to be used: Lincoln's Inn MS. Misc. 514, ff. 42–3. In so dealing with the Chancery depositions, the Barons were confirming the statements of the practice manuals of the period that depositions from another court (or, indeed, from another cause in Exchequer equity) could only be introduced as evidence by special order of the Court, e.g., T, G., *The Practick Part of the Law* (1681), p. 509.

grandfather. Thus, it was Crane's ejectment at Hill's hands in 1693 that occasioned his suit for relief in Exchequer.[15]

It is not clear why Crane should have chosen to litigate his case in Exchequer, given his earlier success in Chancery and given, too, his desire to use the depositions generated in that action. But it remains now to consider the other documentation available for the case that can be found in the Exchequer equity materials.

To begin with, there are the pleadings (bill and answer) located by searching the bill books for William III's reign – under the county of Suffolk (E 112/742, no. 78, the original bill was filed in Hilary term, 1693–4) accompanied by various interlocutory orders involving the taking of the principal defendant's answer by commission. Then there are the depositions taken by commissioners (named November 22, 1694) at Halesworth, Suffolk on 8 and 15 January 1695 and filed as E 134/6&7Wm3/Hil10.[16] Finally, there are the records of the hearing of 29 November 1695 which was continued and concluded on 7 December (E 162/1, f. 6)[17], with the Court awarding a perpetual injunction in favour of Crane's possession of the disputed rectory. In compensation, Crane was to pay Hill the annuity that Crane had contracted to pay at the time of the original transaction, along with outstanding arrears thereon.[18]

(IV) Clegat v. Kinsey (two suits, and cross bill), 1695–9, estate matters

The previous three searches have illustrated a few of the more common problems that can be encountered in locating materials generated by an individual suit. Clegat v. Kinsey, and the two specimen searches to follow, illustrate some less frequent problems.

Using the lists of documentary exhibits brought into Court by litigants and never retrieved after the suit came to an end (primarily the series lists for E 140 and E 219) can be a profitable way to identify suits of interest, since the description of the material contained in the exhibit often provides a good indication of the nature of the dispute concerned. In this case Nicholas Clegat (a cleric) and Richard Wilcox were acting as executors of the will of Jane Fenwick (died 1694), the widow and executrix of Robert Fenwick (died 1693), a prosperous late seventeenth century London vintner and publican. To be sure, the exhibit material is fragmentary – some accounts of construction work at the tavern of which Fenwick was tenant (the 'Young Devil' near Temple Bar in Fleet Street), a list of witnesses for the case, and a few letters – but enough to tell us that the suit was being litigated in the mid-1690s and that the plaintiffs' two bills of complaint were in all likelihood entered by the clerks as London and

15 Ward's 'report' of Crane v. Hill in Lincoln's Inn MS. Misc. 559, f. 10, printed by W.H. Bryson, 'Equity Reports and Records in Early Modern England', in *Case Law in the Making*, ed. Alain Wijffels, vol. 17/2 of *Comparative Studies in Continental and Anglo-American Legal History* (Berlin, 1997), pp. 73–7.

16 Six men were deposed on behalf of the plaintiff, three (one of them also deposed on behalf of the plaintiff) for the defendant. Their testimony focused on the original conveyance from the defendant to the plaintiff.

17 There is a duplicate entry in E 126/16.

18 The decree at E 126/16, f. 303 is printed in full by Bryson, 'Equity Reports and Records in Early-Modern England', pp. 77. In addition to the other information the decree contains, it lists counsel on both sides – six for Crane (including the then Attorney-General) and four for Hill. It should be noted that in the following year Crane brought suit against Susan Hill (as administratrix to John Hill) and Thomas Ampleford, in a related matter: Lincoln's Inn MS Misc 515, f. 73; E 112/717, Norfolk 185.

Middlesex bills (given the residence of the deceased, the residences of the plaintiffs, and the location of the property in question). In one suit, the executors were suing Sir Thomas Kinsey (an even more prominent London vintner and the deceased Fenwick's uncle), the widow Anne Leake, and the gentleman Robert Bird; in the other, the two executors were simply suing Kinsey.

Searching for the rest of the documentation for this suit proved a frustrating exercise, above all because repeated searches of the bill books failed to turn up any trace of either of the two bills filed by Clegat and Wilcox in Hilary 1695, though the search did yield the record of a cross bill filed by Kinsey in Michaelmas 1695 against the two executors and Leake, Bird, and the widow Penelope Aven (London and Middlesex, no. 851 of the reign of William III). However, this bill, too, poses a problem since a clerical note in the bill book (IND 1/16834) indicates that it is 'not on the file'.[19] We have here, then, a striking case of clerical laxity – first, the loss of the two main bills, and secondly, the (?later) loss of the cross bill.

Nonetheless, it is still possible to trace the course of the litigation from the filing of the bills through their hearing, and so find out the outcome of these suits. Depositions taken before the Barons survive in E 133/36/5 and E 133/36/6 (Clegat is a sufficiently unusual surname to search the 'alphabet' for E 133 via the computer catalogue); three for the defendant, taken in February–June 1696 and ten for the plaintiff between October 1695 and June 1696 (including Wilcox being examined in his capacity as executor). For the most part, they focus on the financial dealings between Fenwick and Kinsey, and reveal, incidentally, how much the employees and friends of the deceased Fenwick and his late widow Jane knew about Fenwick's extensive dealings with his uncle.

After the last of the depositions was taken, a hearing was moved and ordered, with the two suits to be considered together, for Michaelmas term 1696.[20] And on 7 November 1696 it was also agreed that Kinsey's cross bill should be taken up with the two original suits (E 161/58, f. 10).

The upshot was generally favourable from the standpoint of Fenwick's executors. In the first place, Kinsey's cross bill was dismissed insofar as it related to the disputed 'Young Devil Tavern' lease, and thereafter it disappears from the record. The judgement on the second bill upheld Fenwick's lease of that tavern. And with respect to the third bill, Kinsey was ordered to account before the Deputy Remembrancer for debts the Court found that he owed to the deceased Fenwick.[21]

(V) Stanton v. Thompson et al., 1694–7, title to land

Proceedings on the Stanton case were first encountered among Chief Baron Ward's notes of hearings. In this instance, the suit was between the widow Mary Stanton and James Thompson and his wife Elizabeth; Elizabeth was the sister of Mary's recently-married and even more

---

19 This annotation was probably the work of the nineteenth-century sorters who created the modern portfolios. In addition, Kinsey was suing Clegat, Wilcox and others in Chancery: C 33/285, f. 18v, Nov. 30, 1695 with Master's report of May 27.

20 Two witnesses were deposed for both sides, the couple Edward and Grace Hindmarsh; he worked in the Six Clerks' Office of the Court of Chancery.

21 See also Lincoln's Inn MS. Misc. 514, f. 152 (23 Nov. 1696).

recently-deceased husband Thomas Stanton. At issue was title to land in Aldington, Kent, allegedly 'strictly' settled before his death in 1691 by Thomas Stanton on trustees for the benefit of Elizabeth Thompson and, after her death, her son.

As Mary Stanton was a London resident, the bill books for London were first searched, but all that could be found (in the portion of the William III and Anne bill book) were two sets of answers to Mary Stanton's bill of complaint – answers listed in the book as 'answers without bills' (giving the defendant's name first) under file numbers 2070 as 'Thompson v. Stanton' (sworn 6 June 1694) and 2072 as 'Nash v. Stanton' (sworn 9 July 1694, Samuel Nash 'merchant' being another of the defendants in his capacity as a trustee under Thomas Stanton's alleged settlement of May 1691). These answers supplied some of the information as to what was at issue in this dispute, and the depositions located via the E 133 alphabet (searched on the computer catalogue) at E 133/117/38 and E 133/117/39 supplied much of the rest.

It was then decided to search in the Kent section of the bill books, on the grounds that the property in dispute was situated there, but no bill of the expected date could be located. However, for the later date of Easter 1697, a bill of complaint by Mary Stanton, widow of London, against James and Elizabeth Thompson and others, was located and traced to the portfolio E 112/663, no. 242.

Putting these materials together with the other entries in the Court's records (particularly useful are the entries in E 126/16 since they recapitulate the proceedings in outline), the following story emerges from the plaintiff's side. Thomas Stanton, unmarried, allegedly made a deed of settlement on his sister and her son after her in July 1691; but late that year he married the plaintiff, and by the power reserved to him under the earlier settlement, settled the property as his new wife's jointure, confirming the arrangement by deed in April 1692, thereby postponing the claims of the Thompsons. By contrast, the defendants alleged a settlement on Elizabeth Thompson and her son made in May 1691 which contained no reserved power to make a jointure.

When Stanton died in 1693 his wife kept possession of the Aldington land. However, in early 1694, at the Lent assizes at Maidstone, the Thompsons (in a surprise move) sued for possession of the land at common law in an action of ejectment and were awarded possession upon trial on the strength of the alleged settlement of May 1691. In response, the widow Stanton proceeded against the Thompsons (along with the trustees under the alleged settlement) in an Exchequer equity complaint (the 1694 bill not located), having convinced the Court that she was destitute and hence qualified to proceed *in forma pauperis*.[22] Depositions on both sides were taken in January 1695 before Baron Lechmere,[23] and at the subsequent hearing before the Barons on 30 May 1695, the dispute was referred to a trial of law at the Middlesex sittings (with a Baron of the Exchequer presiding) over the question of the authenticity of the deeds submitted as proofs by the defendants (E 126/16, ff. 276-77).[24]

This trial produced a verdict in favor of the defendants (E 162/1, f. 1, 24&31 Oct. 1695) but Stanton's counsel was able to convince the Barons that the outcome was erroneous, and a

---

22 Only a handful of petitions for the status of *in forma pauperis* survive for the 1690s, and there is nothing from this case in E 185/16.

23 Five witnesses were deposed for the Thompsons in January 1695; 14 were deposed for the widow Stanton between October 1694 and January 1695.

24 No corresponding entry can be found in E 162/1.

new trial was ordered with 'a good jury of Middlesex' in Michaelmas term 1696 (E 161/58, f. 129).[25] In the event, however, the trial was held at the bar of the Exchequer in November 1696 with a verdict for the plaintiff. The Barons then (E 126/16, ff. 368–9, 16 Dec. 1696) ordered the widow Stanton to be put in possession of the premises and the Thompsons to account before the Deputy Remembrancer for their profits during the time of their possession.[26]

The widow was duly restored in late 1696, yet the following Easter term she found herself back in the Court of Exchequer and again suing the Thompsons and alleged confederates (E 112/663, no. 242). Essentially, her complaint now was that Thompson had failed to satisfy her for the profits of Aldington during his occupancy. Thompson's answer (sworn 8 June 1697, and made with his wife) was rather a rather pathetic one. While his sister-in-law had been able to conduct her first suit at relatively minimal expense *in forma pauperis* (and had gained the same privilege in the present litigation), he had been reduced to insolvency and ended up a prisoner for debt in King's Bench prison. Hence his failure to account. But the widow did not slacken her pursuit, and eventually the defendant was attached for failure to satisfy the decree (a judgement for £105) and also to pay his sister-in-law's legal costs. Thus, the last we hear of Thompson is the Court's committal of him to Fleet Prison on 19 May 1699 (E 131/10, no. 143), leaving the widow as yet unsatisfied.[27]

(VI) Hutchins and Hale v. Dawe et al. (and associated litigation), 1693–8, competing claims on a bankrupt's assets

This dispute centres on the competition for a bankrupt's assets, those of a Somerset clothier by name of Joseph Lovell. Traces of the case were first encountered in some of the depositions it generated, as preserved in E 134 (country depositions), but there were several significant complications that had to be overcome in the search for the other records of the proceedings in this litigation.

In the first place, the depositions at E 134/6W&M/Mich 35 (22 Oct. 1694), E 133/71/27 (22/11 and 1/12 1694), and E 134/7W&M/Hil24 (23 Jan. 1696) themselves suggest that there might have been two separate suits brought by the plaintiffs – Richard Hutchins a merchant, and Richard Hale (both of Frome Selwood, Somerset) – against a variety of defendants, chief of whom was one Edmund Dawe, an attorney of Frome. But a search of the bill books for the appropriate years brought up only one seemingly relevant bill of complaint – E 112/733, no. 267 – filed in Trinity term 1695, that is, before the third set of depositions was taken but well after the first and second set of depositions had been sworn.

Further light on the proceedings was cast by the pleadings in this file. These included a bill of complaint filed as a bill of 'revivor' – a revival of an earlier suit 'abated' (interrupted) by the death of the principal original defendant, the attorney Edmund Dawe. The defendants now named were Dawe's executors (his wife Anne and his son, another Edmund, confusingly).

---

25 The entry is paralleled in E 127/20. A 'good jury', in the Barons' usage, appears to have been a more than ordinarily qualified panel in terms of economic standing (i.e., a 'special' jury). It is also worth remarking that Stanton, though suing *in forma pauperis*, had four counsel arguing on her behalf at the key hearing of 31 Oct. 1695 (E 162/1, f. 1); the defendant appears to have had to be content with one.

26 The entry is paralleled in E 162/1.

27 E 127/20 has no entries for this or for the preceding term; there is an entry in E 161/59.

Attached to the 1695 bill of complaint was the answer, dated July 1693, of Edmund Dawe senior, in refutation of the claims of the original complaint. What appears to have happened is that the original bill (along with Dawe's answer to it), if ever filed, was taken off the file when the bill of revivor was brought in, and in turn the answer to the first bill was then attached to the bill of revivor while the original bill was discarded. So on the one hand, no bill of complaint for the original suit can be located, but on the other hand the terms of the original bill can be reconstructed from the extant pleadings at E 112/733, no. 267.

Nor do the clerical complications of the record end with the displacement of the original bill of complaint and the relocation of the answer to it. For in the entry book for orders for 1693 (E 127/18, f. 102), there is an entry for 24 October 1693 ordering that the plaintiffs' exceptions to the substance of Dawe's answer be heard the following Saturday.[28] The text of these exceptions do not survive as part of the pleadings (presumably having gone the way of the original bill) but Dawe's response to the exceptions, his 'further answer' of 19 December 1693 does survive, but not among the pleadings of the case. Rather, it was located, in the course of another search, as a stray among the London and Middlesex pleadings in the category of 'answers without bills' (E 112/712, no. 2096, another victim of the dismantling of the original file).

Having read through what survives of the pleadings and the three sets of depositions, the nub of the dispute is quite clear[29]. This is, that Hutchins and Hale, two among the various creditors of Lovell who secured a commission of bankruptcy against him from the Court of Chancery in May 1692, were attempting to reclaim various of Lovell's assets that they asserted were in Dawe's possession as a result of a scheme that Dawe ('the penman and contriver of the said matter') had cooked up with Lovell to defraud his creditors, save some of Lovell's assets for him, and unjustly enrich Dawe.[30] The Dawe–Lovell arrangement was memorialized under an indenture of September 1691 which purported to give Dawe all of Lovell's assets in return for the sum of £244. Among these assets was a leasehold property in Somerset (a recent and as yet uncompleted purchase by Lovell from one George Prater and Prater's kinswoman, Anne the wife of Thomas Pickfatt) that was perhaps the most valuable of Dawe's acquisitions.

The plaintiffs alleged that as part of Dawe's machinations, and in particular to frustrate the commissioners of bankruptcy and 'to give colour' to his own claims, Dawe had launched a suit in Michaelmas 1692 purporting to 'quiet his title' in that property by suing Thomas and Anne Pickfatt. (The records of the Dawe–Pickfatt litigation survive in E 112/732, no. 144 (Mich. 1692) and no. 189 (Easter 1694); depositions at E 134/5W&M/East15).

Resolving this tangle of claims and counter-claims upon the assets of Joseph Lovell was a complicated task. After reviewing the depositions and hearing counsel for both sides, the Barons in July 1696 ordered that the Dawe claim to the leasehold property be put to trial at

---

28 There is no parallel entry in E 161.

29 Among the deponents was none other than the bankrupt Lovell, now resident in East Anglia, who was called as one of the Dawes' witnesses: E 133/71/27.

30 The quotation is from the bill of revivor.

common law (E 162/1, f. 39, 10 July 1696).[31] However, the process of arranging the trial was complicated by the defendants' delaying tactics, and it was not until late in the year that the case went to a jury before the Chief Baron presiding at the Middlesex sessions (E 161/58, f. 2, 23 Nov. 1696).[32]

The jury verdict was decisively against the defendants' claims: all that the deceased Edmund Dawe had claimed to have received of Lovell's property under the alleged indenture of September 1691, the jury held, should go to the plaintiffs. In turn the Court, accepting the trial outcome, ordered that the Dawes should account before the Deputy Remembrancer for all of Lovell's chattels in their possession for benefit of the creditors and that the plaintiffs be given possession of the disputed leasehold property (subject to paying the Pickfatts the £100 of the purchase price still outstanding) (E 126/16, ff. 388–89, 10 Dec. 1696).[33]

However, it was to take another year before the Deputy Remembrancer's account was compiled, reviewed, and approved by the Court, with the defendants ordered to pay for (or restore) approximately £35 worth of Lovell's goods as well as what must have been substantial costs (E 126/16, ff. 450–51, 6 Dec. 1697).[34] Perhaps, then, it is not surprising that the last we hear of the case is a motion for contempt proceedings moved by the plaintiffs against the defendants in July 1698 for failure to perform the decree of the previous December (E 161/59, f. 184, 20 July 1698).

Clegat v. Kinsey, Stanton v. Thompson, and Hutchins and Hale v. Dawe each, then, illustrates the problem of deficiencies in the record (chiefly losses from and misfilings in E 112) and also how much can be reconstructed by utilizing possible sources – both the depositions (if any) and the substantive content of records of proceedings (both minutes and orders). At the same time, the Hutchins suit illustrates the oft-encountered situation in which a single suit is revealed to be a part of a larger web of litigation which, to a greater or lesser degree, must be unravelled so as to get as full a view as possible of the matter in dispute.

D. Bonuses for Searchers

Let us conclude this discussion of the search process by emphasizing the often unexpected richness of suit materials. This is a point most easily and most usefully made by reference to 'schedules' – accounts and lists attached by one or another parties to their pleadings, usually answers but not infrequently bills. The range of items so listed is very various. Among the potentially more interesting schedules found among the 1685 sets of pleadings from London and Middlesex are a list of debts allegedly owed by Middlesex water customers (Bucknall v. Barton);

---

31 A partial summary of the E 162 minute reads: 'Mr. Strode opens the bill for the plaintiffs, Mr. Keene for defendant opens the answer of Daw, and also Anne Pickfatt's answer. Mr [illegible] for plaintiffs, Mr. Ettricke for defendants. And the assignment of the commission of bankrupts read. [And various answers to specific interrogatories read]. Referred to a trial at law to be tried the next assizes upon this issue: whether the deed of the 2nd of Sept. 1691 was executed by Lovell before he became a bankrupt. The action to be brought in the Office of Pleas of this Court.' There is a briefer entry in E 126/16.

32 There is a parallel entry in E 127/20.

33 There is a parallel entry in E 162/1.

34 There is a parallel entry in E 162/1.

a schedule of clay sold by a Dorset merchant to a London tobacco pipe-maker (Evans v. Smith); both sides' lists of goods and effects left by a sea captain who died on a voyage from Guinea to Barbados (Gowen v. Cope); a schedule of logwood and other items in transactions involving one of the farmers of the Customs (Isaacson v. Shaw); accounts between a Cambridgeshire gentleman and a merchant tailor of Hatton Garden (Percivall v. Webb) with respect to dealings in malt; accounts of Anthony Row, purveyor to Charles II's stables (Row v. Buckle); financial dealings of a onetime Master of the Mint with the moneyers of the Mint (Slingsby v. Anderson); and an inventory of goods seized from a brew house by commissioners of the excise (Wilkins v. Webster). Similarly, among the 1785 London and Middlesex pleadings, we encounter a set of accounts of a friendly society of London porters (Blackaby v. Jones); accounts of a vessel shipping rice from South Carolina to London which was lost at sea (Fraser v. Huxham); the captain's narrative of a cargo ship, the *Success*, which sank in the Delaware on a voyage from Dublin to Philadelphia (Gill v. Galloway); a list of buildings erected by the architects James and Samuel Wyatt utilizing a newly-invented method of slating roofs (Rawlinson v. Wyatt); and lists of musical compositions (including works by one of the Bach family) in two copyright disputes (Rennett v. Longman, Rennett v. Thompson).

How frequently may one expect to encounter schedules? Our investigations suggests such addenda were attached to one or another set of pleadings (and in some instances to more than one pleading in a given suit) in slightly more than one in every six cases. To be more precise, in the 860 sets of pleadings read for this study (the four sample sets and the additional London and Middlesex sets), 154 (or 18.0%) had schedules attached. Breaking down this overall figure by date and locale, as indicated in Table XXII, it becomes apparent that both chronology and geography appear to influence frequency, with the use of schedules growing more common over time but with London and Middlesex pleadings nearly twice as likely as provincial ones to include schedules over the period as a whole.

Table XXII: Schedules attached to Exchequer pleadings (n=860)

	1685	1735	1785	1819	Totals
London/Mdx	34/151 22.5%	6/45 13.3%	49/194 25.3%	13/52 25.0%	23.1%
Other	9/116 7.8%	13/105 12.3%	11/99 11.1%	19/98 19.4%	12.2%
Totals	43/267 16.1%	19/150 12.7%	60/293 20.5%	32/150 21.3%	18.0%

APPENDIX ONE
Costs in Exchequer Equity

Fowler offers four sets of costs. The first consists of plaintiff's costs in a tithe case, the second of defendant's costs (as residual taker) after payment of testator's debts, the third a bill of costs for each side in the cause of a creditor, and the fourth costs involved in contempt process. Reproduced below, from Fowler II, 516–25, is his second set of costs – those of a defendant (as residual taker) after payment of a testator's debts.

Bill of Cofts of a Defendant, intitled to the Refidue, after Payment of Teftator's Debts.

In the Exchequer.

Magdalen Llwyd, widow and executrix of
David Lloyd, Efq. deceafed,
and
John Philipps, gentleman, executor of *Emma Williams,* fpinfter, deceafed, who fued, as well on behalf of himfelf as others, the creditors of *David Llwyd,* Efq. deceafed.

The Defendant *Llwyd's* bill of cofts.

Hilary Term, 1782.[1]

	£.	s.	d.
Warrant to defend,	0	6	8
Appearance, fee, clerk,	0	3	8
Paid for office-copy bill, folio 48, and duty,	2	6	3
Clofe copy,	0	8	0
Term, fee, folicitor,	0	6	8
Letters and porters,	0	3	0
	3	14	3

Brought

Bill of Cofts.   **517**

	£.	s.	d.
Brought over, - -	3	14	3

Michaelmas Term, 1782.

	£.	s.	d.
Perufing and confidering bill, and fending inftructions to move for time to anfwer, and for dedimus, -	0	6	8
Brief to counfel, - -	0	2	6
To counfel, - -	0	10	6
Drawing order, ingroffing duty, and paid regifter entry, - -	0	5	2
Term fee, - - -	0	10	0
Letters and porters, - -	0	3	0
Attending defendant feveral times, and taking inftruction for anfwer,	0	6	8
Clofe copy, bill to lay before counfel, with anfwer, - -	0	8	0
Drawing the fame, folio 43, -	1	2	6
Fair copy for counfel, -	0	7	2
Clofe copy defendant's marriage fettlement to lay before counfel,	0	13	4
Paid counfel to fettle and fign, -	2	2	0
To his clerk, - -	0	2	6
Agent's attendance with anfwer, and calling for the fame, -	0	6	8
Carriage per coach to London, and back to the country, - -	0	3	0
	11	3	7

5 1 8   *Bill of Cofts.*

	£.	s.	d.
Brought over, – –	11	3	7

Hilary Term, 1783.

Commiffion to take anfwer, –	1	1	2
Poftage to the country, –	0	2	0
Term fee, –	0	10	0
Letters and porters, – – –	0	3	0

Vacation following.

Attending Mrs. Llwyd at Berllandowill, to arrange the accounts to be fcheduled to her anfwer, and horfe-hire,	1	1	0
Fair copy anfwer and fchedules for defendant's perufal, –	0	7	2
Ingroffing, – – – –	0	14	4
Parchment and duty, –	0	5	0

_ N. B. Mrs. Llwyd, after the ingrofsment of this anfwer, found there was a miftake in her fchedules.

Michaelmas Term, 1784.

Term fee and porters, – –	0	12	0
Renewing commiffion to take defendant's anfwer, Remembrancer's fee,	0	10	7
Poftage to the country, –	0	3	0
	16	12	10

Brought

Bill of Cofts.   519

	£.	s.	d.
Brought over, - -	16	12	10
Attending at Berllandowill to meet John Lewis, Efq. Mrs. Llwyd's agent, in the arrangement and fettling of Mr. Llwyd's perfonal eftate, to enable him to amend the anfwer, fchedule, and horfe-hire, -	1	1	0
Attending them with my clerk, and fettling the fchedules, and comparing vouchers and receipts with the fchedules of payment, and horfe-hire for both, - -	1	15	0
Fair copy fchedule and anfwer for defendant, - -	0	7	2

Vacation following.

	£.	s.	d.
Drawing notice of taking anfwer and copy, - -	0	5	0
Attending commiffioners to fign the fame,	0	6	8
Serving notice, - - -	0	2	6
Ingroffing anfwer, - -	0	14	4
Parchment and duty, - -	0	5	0
Paid two commiffioners attending at Berllandowill, to take anfwer, and horfe-hire, - -	0	13	4
	22	2	10

Brought

520   *Bill of Cofts.*

	£.	s.	d.
Brought over, - -	22	2	10
Attending Mrs. Llwyd at Berllandowill, with the anfwer ingroffed, and reading over the fame, comparing the feveral fchedules before anfwer was fworn to, and horfe-hire, -	1	1	0
Meffenger therewith to London, -	0	5	0

Hilary Term, 1785.

	£.	s.	d.
Clerk in court attending him to be fworn,	0	3	4
Paid oath, - - -	0	1	0
Filing defendant's anfwer, -	0	2	0
Term fee, - - -	0	10	0
Porters and letters, - -	0	3	0

Michaelmas Term, 1785.

	£.	s.	d.
Term fee, - -	0	10	0
Office-copy replication, folio 3, and duty, - - -	0	2	9
Appearance to rejoin, - -	0	3	4
Rejoinder, duty, and filing, -	0	7	10
Attending ftriking commiffioners names for examination of witneffes,	0	6	8
Porters and letters, - -	0	3	0
	27	1	9

Brought

Bill of Cofts.   521

	£.	s.	d.
Brought over, - -	27	1	9

Hilary Term, 1786.

	£.	s.	d.
Drawing draft, brief of pleadings, and depofitions, folio 541, -	5	17	6
Two fair copies, containing twenty brief fheets, - -	5	0	0
To Mr. Williams, with his brief,	2	2	0
To his clerk, - -	0	2	6
Attending him, - -	0	6	8
Attending court pleadings, opened teftator's original will, produced and read, but the hearing adjourned to next term, clerk and folicitor,	0	13	4
Coach-hire with papers, -	0	2	0
Term fee and letters, -	0	13	0

Eafter Term, 1786.

	£.	s.	d.
Term fee, -	0	10	0
Refrefhing fee, - -	1	1	0
His clerk, - -	0	2	6
Attending him, - -	0	6	8
Attending court caufe in paper, and ordered to ftand over, clerk and folicitor, - -	0	13	4
Porters and letters, - -	0	3	0
	44	15	3

Bill of Cofts.

	£.	s.	d.
Brought over, - -	44	15	3

N. B. Defendant Magdalen Llywd died, and caufe was revived againft David Edward Lewes Lloyd, Efq. her execu- tor.

Eafter Term, 1788.

Term fee, - -	0	10	0
Warrant to defend, - -	0	6	8
Appearance and fee, - -	0	3	8
Porters and letters, - -	0	3	0

Trinity Term, 1788.

Term fee, - -	0	10	0
Copy bill of revivor, folio 12, and duty,	0	11	0
Clofe copy, - -	0	1	10
Porters and letters, - -	0	3	0

Michaelmas Term, 1788.

Term fee, - -	0	10	0
Refrefhing fee, - -	1	1	0
To his clerk, - -	0	2	6
Attending him, - -	0	6	8
Attending court caufe in paper,	0	13	4
Coach-hire with papers, -	0	2	0
The like, - -	0	15	4
	50	15	3

Brought

Bill of Cofts. **523**

	£.	s.	d.
Brought over,	50	15	3
The like,	0	15	4
The like, caufe heard,	0	15	4
Court fees,	0	4	6
Copy minutes,	0	5	0
Attending Mafter paffing decree,	0	6	8
Porters,	0	2	0

Michaelmas Term, 1789.

	£.	s.	d.
Term fee and letters,	0	13	0
Attending plaintiff's warrant,	0	6	8
Attending plaintiff's warrant,	0	6	8
Paid for office-copy, plaintiff's charge, folio,	0	13	4
Perufing the executor's accounts and the pleadings, and taking inftructions to draw the executor's difcharge,	0	13	4
Drawing difcharge of defendant, Magdalen Llwyd, on account of the perfonal eftate, folio 27, and copy,	0	13	6
Copy thereof for the Mafter,	0	4	6
Warrant on leaving the fame copy and fervice,	0	3	0

Eafter Term, 1791.

	£.	s.	d.
Term fee and letters,	0	13	0
Attending warrant on plaintiff's charge,	0	6	8
	57	2	7

524   *Bill of Cofts.*

	£.	s.	d.
Brought over, - -	57	2	7
Summons on defendant's charge, copy, and fervice, - -	0	3	0
Like fummons, copy, and fervice,	0	3	0
Attending plaintiff's fummons to tax cofts, - - -	0	6	8
Drawing bill of cofts and copy,	1	0	0
Summons to tax defendant's cofts, copy, and fervice, - -	0	3	0
Another fummons to tax defendant's cofts, copy, and fervice, -	0	3	0
Attending taxing defendant's cofts,	0	6	8
Clerk in court, - -	0	3	4

Trinity Term, 1791.

	£.	s.	d.
Term fee and letters, - -	0	12	0
Summons on defendant's difcharge, copy, and fervice, - -	0	3	0
Attending thereon, - -	0	6	8

Eafter Term, 1792.

	£.	s.	d.
Term fee and letters, - -	0	13	0
Summons to tax defendant Llwyd's cofts, copy, and fervice, - -	0	3	0
Attending thereon, and clerk in court,	0	10	0
	61	18	11

Brought

Bill of Costs. 525

	£.	s.	d.
Brought over,	61	18	11
Perusing draft Master's report,	0	6	8
Attending to settle the same,	0	6	8
Allocatur,	0	10	0

Michaelmas Term, 1792.

	£.	s.	d.
Term fee, order served for confirming report, and letters,	0	13	0
Attend to receive defendant's costs,	0	6	8
	64	1	11
	24	7	11
	39	14	0

Bill

APPENDIX TWO
Samples and Selections of Exchequer Pleadings and Suits

Information on process and procedure, duration of suits, subject-matter of suits, status or occupation and residence of litigants, and related matters has been derived from the following samples and selections of sets of pleadings/suits. All told, the pleadings of 860 suits were read (Groups I–III); of these 300 (Group II, a subset of Group I) were traced along with the 258 Ward cases in Group IV.

Group I. Samples of Pleadings: n=600 (300 in II)

Four chronological samples were used. Taking as guidelines the county by county distribution of suits as recorded in the bill books for the decades in question, 150 sets of pleadings were selected and read for the years 1685–6 (1 James II), 1734–5 (8 George II), 1784–5 (25 George III), and 1818–9 (58 George III). In other words, if 30% of the suits for the 1680s recorded in the bill books were filed as London and Middlesex suits and 10% as Norfolk suits, our sample 1685–6 would have included 45 (30% of 150 total) London and Middlesex suits and 15 (10% of 150) Norfolk suits for the year 1685–6, and so on for the rest of the country and Wales. (A calendar of these 600 pleadings, along with the material gathered for Group II below is published in volume 278 [2000] by the List and Index Society.)

Group II. Tracing Sample Suits: n=300 (all in I)

Two of the four samples of pleadings (1685–6 and 1818–9) were used to trace each of the suits included to their final stage of litigation. Thus, 300 of the suits in the total of 600 pleadings were traced in this fashion.

Group III: London and Middlesex pleading (n=345, of which 85 are also in Group I and 34 of those [from 1685] are also in Group II)

For the years 1685–6 and 1784–5 the pleadings for all London and Middlesex suits were read. About a quarter of these were already included in the samples in Group I, and of this quarter somewhat less than half were included in the traced sample suits of Group II. (A calendar of these 345 pleadings is published by the London Record Society, volume 35, 2000.)

Group IV: Ward suits at hearing stage (n=258; no overlap with any other grouping)

Using the Ward MSS. in Lincoln's Inn Library, 258 cases slated for hearings between Michaelmas 1695 and Trinity 1697 were traced both backwards to their inception (pleadings) and forward to their end (conclusion or abandonment).

APPENDIX THREE
Exchequer Equity 'Reports' and Decrees, 1650–1800

There are relatively few Exchequer equity 'reports' of the Barons' legal opinions, either in print (reprinted in vol. 145 of *The English Reports*) or in manuscript for the period 1650–1800. The principal reporters included in *The English Reports* volume and the dates of the cases covered are (1) Thomas Hardres (Baron of the Exchequer), 1655–70; (2) William Bunbury, 1713–41; and Alexander Anstruther, 1792–5. In addition, occasional Exchequer equity cases appear in the reports of Richard Freeman and Sir John Comyns (*The English Reports*, vols. 22 and 92).

The principal manuscript reports, partly duplicating but also considerably adding to the number of the printed cases (and occasionally offering a fuller account than in print), are (in rough date order):

British Library Hargrave MS. 70 (Chief Baron Samuel Dodd's reports, 1689–1713);
Lincoln's Inn MS. Misc. 559 (Chief Baron Edward Ward's reports, 1695–7);
Lilly Library (Univ. of Indiana) MSS. 1139–41 (Baron Robert Price's reports, 1702–10);
Harvard Law School MS. 1216 (anon., 1714–29);
Harvard Law School MS. 1109 (anon., 1720–26);
Lilly Library (Univ. of Indiana) MS. (anon., 1740–44);
Lincoln's Inn MSS. Misc. 1003–4 (Baron Charles Clark, 1742–4).

After 1800, reporting of Exchequer equity decisions explodes exponentially. The reporters, of whom George Price is the most prolific, are numerous, and the last four decades of the Court's equitable activity takes up a good portion of volumes 146 to 150 of The English Reports (with these reporters usually also reporting revenue cases and the growing volume of common law cases handled by the Exchequer).

The reports have been read for a variety of purposes – partly for questions of substance, partly for the many points of procedure that are raised, partly by way of comparison with the 860 cases drawn upon in the handbook. Thus, when reference is made, for example, at footnotes 10 and 19 of Chapter Two, to subject-matter distribution in the reports, it is the pre-1800 reports, both printed and manuscript, from which those numbers are derived. Similarly, when reference is made in such discussion to subject-matter distribution in the Court's decrees, the reference is to the pre-1800 decrees as entered in E 126 (specifically 65 decrees for the year 1685–6, 70 for 1735–6, and 68 for 1785–6, for a total of 203.

BIBLIOGRAPHY

I   printed sources: Exchequer equity records
II   other printed works, pre-1850
III secondary works
IV   printed guides to Exchequer equity records
V   manuscript materials relating to Exchequer equity located outside the PRO

Note that in compiling this bibliography, I have excluded materials dealing only with the other 'sides' of Exchequer's judicial business (common pleas and revenue cases) and have included material treating equity and equity courts broadly as well as works on or relating to Chancery where they seemed relevant to understanding Exchequer equity doctrine and practice.

I. Printed Sources: Exchequer and other equity records

Bridgeman, Richard Whalley, *An Analytical Digested Index of the Reported Cases in the Several Courts of Equity* (1805)

Eagle, Francis King, *A Collection of the Reports of Cases . . . Relating to Tithes* (4 vols., 1826)

The English Reports (1900 ff.): vols. 1–3 contain House of Lords cases for the 17th-18th centuries; vols. 145–50 contain printed Exchequer cases for the period

Gwillim, Henry, *A Collection of Acts and Records of Parliament, with Reports of Cases . . . the Courts of Law and Equity, Respecting Tithes* (4 vols., 1821)

Kirkby, William, *Rules and Orders of the Court of Exchequer Relative to the Practice of the King's Remembrancer's Office* (1794)

The Manuscripts of the House of Lords [printed by the Historical Manuscript Commission and continued by the House of Lords from 1694 to 1718; thereafter, reference must be had to the printed *Lords' Journals* and to the manuscript materials in the House of Lords Record Office]

Martin, Adam, *Index to various Repertories, Books of Orders, and Decrees, and other Records Preserved in the Court of Exchequer* (1819)

Lord Nottingham's Chancery Cases (2 vols., Selden Society 73 & 79: 1957 & 1962), ed. D. E. C. Yale

Lord Nottingham's 'Manual of Chancery Practice' and 'Prolegomena of Chancery and Equity' (1965), ed. D. E. C. Yale

Price, George, *Reports of Cases . . . in the Court of Exchequer* [from Easter 54 George III through Michaelmas 56 George IV] (13 vols., 1816–30)

Price, George, *A Treatise on the Law of the Exchequer* (1830)

Rayner, John, *Cases at Large, concerning Tithes; in particular those of the Exchequer* (3 vols., 1789)

St. German's Doctor and Student (Selden Society 91: 1974), ed. J. L. Barton

St. German on Chancery and Statute (Selden Society, supplementary series 6: 1986), ed. John A. Guy

Sanders, G. W., *The Orders of the High Court of Chancery* (1845): the best edition for the period up to the date of its publication

Western, Thomas George, *Cases relating to the tithes of the City of London determined in the Several Courts of Law and Equity* (1823)

Wood, Hutton, *A Collection of Decrees of Exchequer in Tithe Causes, From the Usurpation to the Present Time* (4 vols., 1798–9)

II. Other printed works pre-1850

(A) works relating to reform of the law and of Chancery

(B) manuals written for practitioners and treatises on doctrine

Call numbers are for the British Library, unless otherwise indicated; Wing references are to the printed Short Title Catalogue for 1640–1700; Eighteenth Century Short Title Catalogue references (ESTC) are from the CD-ROM version (some of these items not given locations in England are available on microfilm from Resource Publications' 'Eighteenth-Century Short Title' series). Wing and ESTC references are usually provided when no British Library copy exists or, if in the catalogue, could not be produced by the Library. The Law Society Library and Lincoln's Inn Library also have broad holdings, and, for mid-seventeenth century items, the London Library has proved useful as well.

A. *Reform and related questions*

Animadversions upon the present laws of England (1750), 518 h.14(4)

Certain Quaeres for the Publike Good, Concerning the Avoiding of Multitudes of Unnecessary Orders, Delays, Charges and Troubles in Courts called English Courts or Courts of Equity (1647), Wing C1747 (BL: Thomason tracts)

Considerations touching the dissolving or taking away the Court of Chancery (1653), 518 b.3(3) [London Library, Pamph. 626: endorsed 'by Fabian Phillips who was afterwards publicly thanked for it by Lenthall']

Continuance of the High Court of Chancery Vindicated (1654), E809(2)

Cooper, Charles P., *A Brief Account of some of the most important Proceedings in Parliament relative to the . . . Court of Chancery* (1828), and see *Parliamentary Papers*

D., L. *Exact Relation of the Proceedings of the late Parliament Dissolved, 12th Dec. 1653* (1654), E729(6)

An Essay on the Amendment and Reduction of the Laws of England (1724) – see below, *Law Quibbles*

Edwin Field, *Observations of a Solicitor on the Defects . . . of the Equity Courts* (1840), 1382 d.24

Fitzsimmondes, Joshua, barrister, *Free and Candid Disquisitions, on the nature and execution of the Laws of England, Both in Civil and Criminal Affairs* (1751), 115, f.34

Hale, Matthew, 'Considerations touching the Amendment or Alteration of the Law', *A Collection of Tracts Relative to the Laws of England*, ed. Francis Hargrave, I (1787), 253–89

Hints of the Pending Scheme for Relieving the Suitors in Courts of Equity (1830), 1383 e.11

House of Commons Sessional Papers of the Eighteenth Century, ed. Shelia Lambert, vols. 133–34 (1975) 'Reports from the Select Committee Appointed to Inquire into the State of the Public Records' (1800), and see *Parliamentary Papers*

House of Lords Journals 72 (1840), Appendix 3, 'Administration of Justice Bill', pp. 117–53 also printed as 'Select Committee of House of Lords on bill intituled Act for Facilitating Administration of Justice', *Parliamentary Papers* 1840, 500, xv)

Law Quibbles (1724), 6146, f.20

Leach, William, *An Abatement of most of the motions and orders in Chancery* (1652), 518 i.3(10)

Leigh, Edward, 'gent', *Second Considerations Concerning the high court of Chancery*, 1658, London Library, Pamph. 626/9 – this is a virtual reprint of 13 pp. of his earlier *Some Considerations* (below)

Norbury, George, 'Abuses and Remedies of Chancery' (c.1626, addressed to Lord Keeper Williams) in *A Collection of Tracts Relative to the Laws of England*, ed. Francis Hargrave, I (1787), 425–48

Observations concerning the Chancery with some Proposals for the Redress of the Inconveniences in the Practices thereof (1653: *sic*, but after the Chancery Ordinance), E821(12) [dated Jan. 1 1654[–5] by Thomason]

Observations upon the dilatory . . . proceedings in the Court of Chancery in relation to the bill

now depending . . . for lessening the number of attorneys and solicitors (1701) Cambridge University Library, Bb* 10.39/9

Parliamentary Papers (and see *House of Commons, House of Lords*)

1810–11 (244) iii Causes of delay in Chancery

1812 (273) ii Causes of delay in Chancery, 2nd report

1812–13 (28 & 29 & 32) xiii Accounts of decrees . . . causes . . . bills in Chancery

1822 (125) xi Emoluments in the Courts of Exchequer and Exchequer Chamber

1826 (143) xv, xvi Royal Commission on practice in Chancery

1826/27 (70) xvii Return of the number of bills filed in the Exchequer Court, 1820–26

1836 (370) xlvii State of business in Chancery and Exchequer 1750–1835

(Philostratus Philodemius), *Seasonable Observations on a late book intituled System of the Law, so far as it relates to the High Court of Chancery and the Fees and Proceedings thereof* (1653)

The Present State of the Practice and Practisers of the Law (1750)

Proceedings of the Barons of Exchequer . . . for Tythes and Oblations (1705), 4152, f.23 (26)

Proposals concerning the Chancery (1650/51), E593(19) and 518 i.3(7) (reprinted as *Proposals presented to the hon. committee for regulating courts of justice on 18 Oct. 1650*, E615(21))

Proposals humbly offered to the Honourable the House of Commons, for remedying the great charge and delay of suits at law and in equity (1706), 3rd edn. (1724), 515 h.14(5)

The Representative of diveres well-affected . . . touching the present laws, and government . . . with xxxix new proposals (1649), 518 i.3(6)

Some Considerations concerning the High-Court of Chancery (?1654), 1490 d22 (and see above under Edward Leigh)

Tancred, Christopher, *Essay for a general regulation of law* (1727)

View of the Regulations of the Chancery, A, (1640 and 1654), 518 b.33(2)

[Williams, Walter (MT barrister)], *Reasons Humbly offered . . . the Commons of England, . . . for their speedy endeavour to Regulate the Proceedings of the Court of Chancery with a Proposal how it may be legally done without an act of Parliament* (endorsed 'in case the bill now before them should not pass') (1693–99?), 816 m.15(62)

B. *Practice manuals and treatises on doctrine*

Ballow, Henry, *A treatise of equity* (1737), 6192 aa.1 [for 1793 and later editions, see Fonblanque, John, *A Treatise of Equity*]

Barton, Charles, *An Historical treatise of a Suit in Equity* (1796), 518 k.6(3) or 228 h.4

Beames, John, *Elements of Pleas* (1818), 511 c.15

Beames, John, *Doctrine of the Courts of Equity re Costs* (1822), Law Society Library

Bohun, William, *Cursus Cancellaria* (2nd edn., 1723), 883 h.17

Bohun, William, *Practising attorney: or, lawyer's office* (2nd edn. 1726), Law Society Library [see also Richardson, Robert, *Practicing Attorney: or, Lawyer's office* (4th edn., 1737); and see *Practicing Attorney and Solicitor: Containing the Lawyer's Office in Equity* (4th edn., 1737), both at Law Society Library]

[Boote, Richard] *The Solicitor's Practice in the High Court of Chancery Epitmized* (5th edn., 1782)

[Booth, William], *The Compleat Solicitor Performing His Duty* (1st edn., 1666), Guildhall Lib. AN15.3.37

Brown, William, *Praxis Almae Curia Cancellariae* (first edn., 1694) 1714 edn. at 513 b.2

Brown, William, *A Compendium of the several branches of practice in the Court of the Exchequer* (same as his *The Practice in the Court of Exchequer in its several branches* and also *The Practice of his Majesties Court of Exchequer . . . as to Proceedings in Equity by English bill*) various dates 1688–1725 but all versions appear to have same (unrevised) contents, principally William Byde's 'Compendium' (early 17th c.) and various

Exchequer equity forms and precedents

Collection of Interrogatories for the Examination of Witnesses in Courts of Equity (2nd edn., 1776), 510 d.21

Complete Attorney (1654), Cambridge University Library

Cunningham, T., *A new treatise on the Laws concerning Tithes* (4th edn., 1777)

Ellis, Charles, *A Treatise on the Pleadings in Suits for Tithes in Equity* (1821)

Equity Pleader's Assistant (Dublin 1796) [mainly Irish]

Fowler, David Burton, *The Practice of the Court of Exchequer, upon Proceedings in equity* (1795), 228, f.26–27

Francis, Richard, *Maxims of Equity* (1727), 509 h.6 [modern reprint edn. of 1978]; and see Roscoe Pound, 'On certain maxims in equity', *Cambridge Legal Essays in Honor of Bond, Buckland, and Kenney* (1926), p. 267

Gilbert, Geoffrey, *Two Treatises on the proceedings in equity, and the jurisdiction of that court* (Dublin 1756–58); and see M. Macnair, 'Sir Geoffrey Gilbert and his Treatises', *Journal of Legal History* 15 (1994), 252–68

Grounds and Rudiment of Law and Equity (1749) Law Society Library

Hake, Edward, *Epieikeia: A Dialogue on Equity in Three Parts*, ed. D. E. C. Yale (1958), and see Raymond B. Marcin, 'Epieikeia: Equitable Lawmaking in the Construction of Statutes', *Connecticut Law Review* 10 (1978), 377

Hands, William, *Solicitor's Assistant in the Court of Chancery* (1809), Law Society Library

Harrison, Joseph, *The Accomplished Practicer in the High Court of Chancery*, (5th edn. 1779), 516 c.55 (Law Society Library has edn. of 1741)

Howard, Gorges Edmond, *A Treatise on the rules and practice of the equity side of the Exchequer in Ireland* (2 vols, 1760), 509 b.12–13

[Jacob, Giles], *The Compleat Chancery Practicer* (1730), 510 d.1–2

Jacob, Giles, *A New Law Dictionary* (1732 and ff.)

Maddock, Henry, *A Treatise on the Principles and Practice of the High Court of Chancery* (2 vols., 1820)

Mitford, John, *A Treatise on the Pleadings in Chancery* (1780), 518 h.15(1)

[Osborne, Peter], *The Practice of the Exchequer Court* (1658), E1928(1)

Parkes, Joseph, *A History of the Court of Chancery* (1828)

Points in Law and Equity...[for] all persons concerned in trade and commerce (Dublin 1793)

Powell, Thomas, *The Attourneys Academy* (1623), C113 b.3

The Practical Register in Chancery (1714), 228 g.31 [reprinted with additions in 1800 by John Wyatt as *The Practical Register in Chancery with the addition of the Modern Case*s]

The Practice of the Court of Chancery of the County Palatine of Durham (1807), 510 d.15

The Practice of the High Court of Chancery Unfolded (1652), E 1292[2]) dated 'Nov. 6, 1651'

Present Practice of the High Court of Chancery 1741 (by a gent. of the Six Clerks' Office), 510 a.33–34

Sanders, Francis Williams, *An Essay on the nature and laws of uses and trusts* (1791), 574 d.10

Sheppard, William, *Faithful Councellor* (1651, 2nd part 1653)

Sheppard, William, *England's Balme* (1656), E1675(2)

Spence, George, *The Equitable Jurisdiction of the Court of Chancery* (2 vols., 1846)

Story, Joseph, *Commentaries on Equity Jurisprudence, as administered in England and America* (1839)

T, G., *Practick Part of the Law: shewing the office of an attorney, and a guide for Solicitors in the Courts of Chancery...* (1681), 883, f. 13

[Turner, Samuel], *Costs in the Court of Chancery; with practical directions and remarks* (1791), 1241 g.5

Turner, Samuel, *Epitome of the Practice of the Equity Side of the Exchequer* (2nd edn., 1806), 1129 i3

Turner, Samuel, *Epitome of the Practice of the*

High Court of Chancery (2nd edn., 1809)

View of the Regulations of the Chancery (1640, 1654), 518 b.33(2)

[Walker, Maynard Chamberlain], *Equity Pleader's Assistant* (1796), King's Inn Library, Dublin

West, William, *Three Treatises, of the second part of Symbolograephia... whereto is annextd another Treatise of Equitie...* (1594), 1586/9026

Williams, William, *Jus Appellandi ad Regum ipsum a Cancellaria* (1683)

Wyatt, John, see *The Practical Register*

III. Secondary Works on the Court of Exchequer, on Equity, and on related topics in Early Modern Legal History (Books, Articles and Dissertations)

In general, the best short guide is John H. Baker, *An Introduction to English Legal History* (3rd edn., 1990), chapter 6. In turn, Baker's bibliography gives the relevant volumes and pages of Sir William Holdsworth's *History of English Law* (16 vols, 1922–66)

More specialized works include:

R. M. Ball, 'Tobias Eden, Change and Conflict in the Exchequer Office, 1672–1698', *Journal of Legal History* 11 (1990), 70–89

R. M. Ball, 'The King's Remembrancer's Office in the eighteenth century', *Journal of Legal History* 11 (1990), 90–113

Bernwood Life and After-Life of a Forest, John Broad and Richard W. Hoyle eds. (Preston, 1997)

Christopher W. Brooks, *Lawyers, Litigation and English Society since 1450* (1998)

William H. Bryson, *The Equity Side of the Exchequer: its Jurisdiction, Administration, Procedures and Records* (1975)

W. H. Bryson, 'Exchequer Equity Bibliography', *American Journal of Legal History* 14 (1970), 333–48

W. H. Bryson, 'Equity Reports and Records in Early-Modern England', *Case Law in the Making The Techniques and Methods of Judicial Records and Law Reports*, ed. Alain

Wijffels (Comparative Studies in Continental and Anglo-American Legal History, vol. 17 [Berlin, 1997]), I, 69–82, and II, 54–84

Allen J. Busch jr., 'Bulstrode Whitelocke and Early Interregnum Chancery Reform', *Albion* 10 (1979), 317–30

A. J. Busch jr., 'The John Lisle Chancery Manuscripts: The "Abridgements" [&] "The Pleas and Demurrer"', *Journal of Legal History* 10 (1989), 317–42

W. A. Champion, 'Recourse to law and the meaning of the great litigation decline, 1650–1750: some clues from the Shrewbury local courts', *Communities and Courts in Britain 1150–1900* (1997), eds. C. W. Brooks and Michael Lobban, pp. 179–98

Christine Churches, '"Equity against a purchaser shall not be": a seventeenth-century case study in landholding and indebtedness', *Parergon* new series 11 (1993), 69–87

C. Churches, '"The most unconvincing testimony": the genesis and historical usefulness of the country deposition in Chancery', *Seventeenth Century,* XI (1996), 209–27

Clyde E. Croft, 'Lord Hardwicke's Use of Precedent in Equity', *Legal Record and Historical Reality* (1989), ed. Thomas G. Watkin, pp. 121–55

James S. Hart, *Justice upon Petition: the House of Lords and the Reformation of Justice 1621–1675* (1991)

Edith G. Henderson, 'Legal rights to Land in the early Chancery', *American Journal of Legal History* 26 (1982), 97–122

Peter Charles Hoffer, *The Law's Conscience Equitable Constitutionalism in America* (1990)

Henry Horwitz, *Chancery Equity Records and Proceedings 1600–1800* (PRO Handbook no. 27, 2nd edn., 1998)

H. Horwitz, 'Chancery's "Younger Sister": the Court of Exchequer and its Equity Jurisdiction, 1649–1841', *Historical Research* 72 (1999), 160–82

H. Horwitz, 'Recordkeepers in the Court of Chancery and their "record" of accomplishment', *Historical Research* 70 (1997), 34–51

H. Horwitz and P. Polden, 'Continuity or Change

in the Court of Chancery in the Seventeenth and Eighteenth Centuries?', *Journal of British Studies* 35 (1996), 24–57

Neil G. Jones, 'The influence of revenue considerations upon the remedial practice of Chancery in Trust Cases 1536–1660', *Communities and Courts in Britain 1150–1900* (1997), eds. C. W. Brooks and Michael Lobban, pp. 99–114

William J. Jones, *The Elizabethan Court of Chancery* (1967)

W. J. Jones, 'Palatine performance in the seventeenth century', *The English Commonwealth 1547–1640* (1979), eds. Peter Clark *et al.*, pp. 189–204

D. Klinck, 'Lord Eldon on Equity', *Journal of Legal History* 20/3 (12/1998), 51–74

Louis A. Knafla, *Law and Politics in Jacobean England The Tracts of Lord Chancellor Ellesmere* (1977)

Marcus Knight, 'Litigants and Litigation in the Seventeenth Century Palatinate of Durham', Cambridge Ph.d. 1990

David Lemmings, *Gentlemen and Barristers: The Inns of Court and the English Bar, 1689–1730* (1990)

Peter McDermott, 'Jurisdiction of the Court of Chancery to Award Damages', *Law Quarterly Review* 108 (1992), 652–73

Nancy A. Mace, 'Haydn and the London Music Sellers: *Forster v. Longman, Broderip*', *Music & Letters*, 77 (1996), 527

Michael Macnair, 'The Law of Proof in Early Modern Equity', D. Phil. Oxford 1991

M. Macnair, 'Common law and statutory imitations of equitable relief under the later Stuarts', *Communities and Courts in Britain 1150–1900* (1997), eds. C. W. Brooks and Michael Lobban, pp. 115–31

Nancy L. Matthews, *William Sheppard: Cromwell's Law Reformer* (1985)

Judith Milhous and R. Hume, 'Eighteenth-century Equity Lawsuits in the Court of Exchequer as a Source for Historical Research', *Historical Research* 70 (1997), 231–46

Craig Muldrew, *The Economy of Obligation* (1998)

R. B. Outhwaite, 'A note on *The Practice of the Exchequer Court, With its several Offices and Officers;* by T.F., *English Historical Review* 81 (1966), 337

Roscoe Pound, 'The Progress of the Law, 1918–1919 – Equity', *Harvard Law Review* 33 (1920), part iii, at pp. 941–42

Wilfrid Prest, 'Law Reform in Eighteenth-Century England', *The Life of the Law* (1993), ed. Peter Birks, pp. 113–23

John Sainty, *Officers of the Exchequer* (List & Index Society, xvii, 1983). And see Lawrence Squibb, 'A Book of All the several Officers of the Court of Exchequer. . .', ed. W. H. Bryson, *Camden Miscellany xxvi* (Royal Historical Society, Camden Society Publications, 4th series, 14, 1975)

Barbara Shapiro, 'Law Reform in Seventeenth Century England', *American Journal of Legal History* 19 (1975), 280–312

Tim Stretton, *Women Waging Law in Elizabethan England* (1998)

R. W. Turner, *The Equity of Redemption* (1931)

Donald Veall, *The Popular Movement for Law Reform* (1970)

Andy Wood, *The Politics of Social Conflict: The Peak Country 1520–1770* (1999)

David Yale, 'The Revival of Equitable Estates in the Seventeenth Century: an Explanation by Lord Nottingham', *Cambridge Law Journal* 16 (1957), 72–86

D. Yale, 'A Trichotemy of Equity', *Journal of Legal History* 6 (1985), 194–200

S. Yeazell, 'Default and Modern Process', *Legal History in the Making* (1991), eds. W. M. Gordon and T. D. Fergus, pp. 125-44

Stephen C. Yeazell, *From Medieval Group Litigation to Modern Class Action* (1987)

IV. Printed guides/calendars to equity records, in addition to those listed in Appendix One

Maurice Beresford, 'The Decree Rolls of Chancery as a Source for Economic History 1547–c.1700', *Economic History Review*, 2nd series 32 (1979), 1–10

A Calendar of Lancashire and Cheshire Exchequer Depositions by Commission 1558–1802, ed. Caroline Fishwick (1885), Ac 8121

Exchequer Depositions by Commission for Somerset 1565–1610, transcribed by E. Dwelly, prepared by Adrian J. Webb (1992), YK1993 a6386

Exchequer Proceedings Concerning Wales in Tempore James I Abstracts of Bills and Answers and Inventory of Further Proceedings, compiled by T. I. Jeffreys Jones (Board of Celtic Studies, Univ. of Wales, History and Law Series no. XV, Cardiff 1955)

Exchequer Proceedings (Equity) Concerning Wales Henry VIII–Elizabeth Abstracts of Bills and Inventory of Further Proceedings, compiled by E. G. Jones (Board of Celtic Studies, Univ. of Wales, History and Law Series, no. IV, Cardiff 1939

Exchequer Special Commisssions of Inquiry, Devon and Somerset, 1560–1846, Ed. Adrian J. Webb (1993), YK1994 a7023

Guy Lawton, 'Using Bernau's Index', 3 parts in *Family Tree Magazine*, VIII, parts 2–4 (12/1991–2/1992), pp. 42–3 in each

Guy Lawton, 'Using Bernau's Notebooks', 3 parts in *Family Tree Magazine*, X, parts 2–4 (12/1994–2/1995), pp. 44, 21, and 15

Samples of Chancery Pleadings and Suits: 1628, 1685, 1735, and 1785 (List & Index Society, vol. 257, 1995), compiled by Henry Horwitz and Charles Moreton

Samples of Exchequer Equity Pleadings and Suits: 1685–86, 1734–35, 1784–85, and 1818–19 (List & Index Society, vol. 278, 2000), compiled by Jessica Cooke and Henry Horwitz

Surrey Cases and Deponents in the Court of Exchequer 1561–1835, compiled by Cliff Webb (West Surrey Family History Society, Record Series 19 [1994]) Document Service Centre: 7326.1038.19

T. Trowles, 'Eighteenth century Exchequer Records as a Genealogical Source', *Genealogists' Magazine* 25 (1995), 93–98

INDEX